MW01087197

MINDSET LIBERATION

BREAKTHROUGH STRATEGIES FOR SUCCESS

by
VITALY SAMONOV

MINDSET LIBERATION

BREAKTHROUGH STRATEGIES FOR SUCCESS

TABLE OF CONTENTS

PART THREE: Mindset For Sucess

PART FOUR: Business Success

PART FIVE: Financial

PART SIX: Lifestyle, Values and Defining Success

NOTE FROM THE AUTHOR

I have read hundreds of books, but only after writing one that I truly see the light.

Hi, my name is Vitaly Samonov and I am an entrepreneur, business and life coach, IT Consultant, and a writer. I love reading. I try to read around at least a hundred books on average a year to provide myself with building blocks for action and creativity.

I work with dozens of clients every year and absolutely love what I do. I love being creative with other businesses and with my own projects. I have been in a successful relationship with my long-term girlfriend and my family whom I strongly consider to be vital to my business and overall life success. I wrote this book to share my experience, knowledge and hard work that is backed with a sense of integrity.

have a passion for genuine contribution to people, charitable causes, technology, education, workplace and this planet. All of these are above monetary goals in the way that makes this world a better place.

I love to read and write and I love working with people on a vast variety of projects that can benefit this world and provide true value to society. I strive to create an overall more meaningful, healthy and fulfilled life. In fact, I love sharing what I have discovered and achieved with others to also help them achieve a well-balanced, happy and meaningful life for themselves, find true success in business and life including relationships, spiritually and personal health.

I personally believe that life should be well rounded and every aspect of it really align with one another. More importantly each area should be developed and invested into in order to achieve true success be it business, financial, philanthropic, spirituality, relationship or health and fitness. I strive to help open human minds for them to see the endless possibilities and help them see the real truth beyond media, formal education and societal norms that anything is possible and it really is up to you to truly make the right choices in life to be the difference that you want to see in the world.

believe that when trained properly the mindset as the number one asset is the key to generating a healthy and sustainable foundation for every aspect of your life.

WE ARE THE CREATORS OF OUR OWN HAPPINESS

How to be happy: my story

DO YOU FEEL LIKE you are in a constant pursuit of satisfaction and keep on wanting to thrive for a higher level of achievement?

Well, I'm here to tell you that it's not a bad thing and that it's the universe's way of persuading us to evolve. I for one have noticed it throughout my life and I am sure you have also at some point as well. You may have found yourself going from a struggling financial state to incredibly successful. With the difference being so dramatic that you would think during the very successful and financially rewarding part of your life, you would be happier.

But it doesn't always happen that way, because by nature we are conditioned to never be fully satisfied. This is so we can continue evolution. Happiness really lies on a chemical level, so we have to make ourselves feel happy. We have free will and awareness with which we can control our whole being and state of mind no matter what the outside circumstances are.

When I was growing up during the fall of communism in Russia the country and financial system was a mess. I calculated that at one point my family lived on less than 20 dollars per month. There were bread and sugar lines for days, freezing weather and we had to wait for public transportation for hours in extreme conditions. Furthermore, there was no hot or sometimes even any water for up to two to three weeks at a time so we had to store water to drink it and boil it to take showers. We even had to can food and store it in the closet for winter.

I remember when the first McDonalds opened when I was 14 years old. I ate about 9 of those dollar hamburgers and chased them down with a milkshake on my friend's birthday. That was one of the most memorable meals of my life.

Compared to the way I live now; thousands of times more financially advanced, I could ask myself, am I happier? Well the answer is that I'm overwhelmingly happy and grateful yes, but so I was back then also. Growing up, I remember being a very happy child and I had incredible friends, teachers and family. I enjoyed playing sports, skiing, skating and playing soccer with friends. My life was about relationships and education. I attended one of the best schools in the city and the level of education was excellent. Teams from our school repeatedly competed on the world level in physics, mathematics and other subjects, we even took second, third and fourth place in the world.

Everything was awesome. My mindset was great, positive, I was always excited - it was inside of me and I could control my happiness level with my mind, because I was constantly grateful for the smallest things! The environment around me has changed dramatically since then. Now I live in San Diego in an incredible place, drive my dream cars, I eat at nice restaurants and do what I want when I want, all thou I still enjoy McDonalds once in a while which brings me back to that glorious day in my childhood, I travel and buy whatever I need. The weather is perfect and I am also incredibly happy all of the time, because I am grateful.

I can honestly say that I could do nothing, or anything I want for the rest of my life and still live a very happy life. To the person reading this, chances are you could do this right now as well if you consciously choose to do so.

So why can't or wouldn't you just start doing what you really desire right now and enjoy your life to the fullest. If I could do that in Russia in the 1980's in such extreme conditions, and even those conditions were paradise compare to what veterans of wars went through, stories I have heard from my grandfather, veteran of WW2 and a Colonel, are way beyond modern person's comprehension and he told those stories with such ease and enthusiasm, there is no reason or excuse why you can't do it now. In fact, it's never been easier. In today's society so many people can make it happen, and at any time you can become happy, successful and live the dream if you choose to think of what you are now and have now is the definition of those things, then you are automatically happy right now. Your life is what you think it is.

In today's connected world, there are overwhelmingly vast amounts of options available to you. You can do freelance work, start a blog, drive an Uber, deliver food, do small gigs, play an instrument at a restaurant, (which I actually used to play piano at a country club in high school, not a bad job for a 16-year-old) walk people's dogs, deliver food, become a consultant on a subject you are good at, or work on any small to big size projects while traveling, teach yourself a certain skill and offer it to others as a service, develop a product and sell it, start a startup get investors and grow it into next Google, should I keep going? With the right attitude and determination you can learn a certain skill and get the job that you want at a company that you want. You can join a philanthropic endeavor of your choice right now if that's what you desire. I have a client who is a Surgeon and he started a company where he travels the world raising money to aid natural disasters, his very demanding job didn't stop him from his other morally high endeavors. It's especially easy to be mobile, make money and provide contribution to the world in many different ways if you are young and without any dependents, but it's never too late to start. Don't use age and having kids as an excuse, please.

Don't hold yourself back and think you have to be a certain way to fit in or appear rich and successful. Just be you. Liberate yourself from thinking you have to be a certain way. The world is your oyster; you can do anything you want. Don't wait till you become "food for worms" as Robert Williams puts it in one of the greatest movies: Dead Poets Society.

The good news is that if you are not completely happy with where your life is, you don't have to do what you are doing right now. Our brain is wired to tell us that we have to continue doing things and working harder in order to survive, but in the modern world especially if you live in a first world country, there are so many things available to you - money, help, resources, people it's all out there for you. All you have to do is show a little effort and ask for help.

If you feel that your life is hard or complex, it is simply because YOU created it that way with unnecessary bills and things you got pushed to buy. With media, salesmen, and people who are telling you that you have to have it to be cool, rich or have status and appear successful, or that you thought it was something you needed. In reality, it does the opposite, purchasing and displaying expensive things makes you less rich and it robs you of time and money. Which you could invest frugally instead into building real wealth like investing in yourself, relationships and your business. Also, if you adopt a minimalist lifestyle for example, you can travel, you can be free and you can do it right now. But if that's not your choice though, that's fine also. Nothing is the way it is, it's only how you think it could be.

I always reflect back on my secret to being happy and vibrant despite the extreme environment during my childhood. It was the decision in my mind to be happy unconditionally combined with gratefulness, despite the outside circumstances. I chose to think positively about things and they were. I believe that if you actually experience such insanely dramatic difference in lifestyles throughout your lifetime, you come to appreciate things and see how life can really be. You see that you can actually be happy and survive with much less than what you have, think you should have, or others have told you, you should have.

In knowing that now, I am always happy and positive, thinking that I have way more than I need, it makes me really grateful, which is a main ingredient in the recipe for happiness. This is one of the not so secrets from my life that I wanted to share and contribute to others because I constantly see people in very stressed, anxious and depressed states who also happen to be living such lavish lifestyles. It seems almost criminal for them not to be satisfied, but it's our nature to always grow, that is the way of evolution. We are imprisoned in a body that is brainwashed by the chemicals in our brain to always try to accomplish and accumulate more, and the more you have the less you appreciate.

So how can the so called rich not be happy then, surely, they have it all. Well like I mentioned earlier, our mind has a tendency to push us into a zone of discontent so that we can thrive to keep evolving. We really all have a choice and if we are consciously aware of this, then we can choose to be happy right now. You have a choice to choose to be happy and you are in control of your thoughts and your destiny. Your inner world is the reality; the outside world is an illusion created by the brain that is accumulated by our receptors. Just like our eyes capture an image of reality, its actually distorted and backwards, but the brain interprets it into a perfect image afterwards. So, interpret reality how you want it to be, make it what you want it to be with your mind. You alone have that power

PART 1

THE EVOLUTION OF THE MIND

THE EVOLUTION OF THE MIND

We are not what we think, rather what we think, we are.

One of my favorite quotes is *"We are not what we think we are, but what we think – we are."* If you truly get this and I mean not just 'wow this is a great sounding statement' but the depth of it applied to reality. Then when you hear it you will be able to tell straight away several situations that you have been in that would be a perfect example of it.

There are different ways to look at this statement and you can attribute a different meaning to just about anything. After all, words are just waves in an elastic medium which are sensed by our receptors and afterwards interpreted by our brain into meaning.

I think of this statement to be a concept generated by our understanding of who we supposed to be, dictated by the conditions of our past, how our brain developed during childhood, current life situation and other influences, versus projecting your thoughts into reality, making them your action and realizing them. In other words, who we think - we will become, not who we already think we have to be. From my real-life experience, this is one of the most core keys to get started on a journey to success and fulfillment. If you truly understand this concept and apply it to reality, then it is one of the first steps.

Also, being confident in what you want to achieve is an extremely important factor in starting your own business. If I didn't have a confident personality, I would never have embarked on the challenges that I have. In fact, you don't have to have that type of personality to begin with. You can become exactly who you really want to and this is actually one of the core concepts of this quote.

So, it's simple, to start a business you need to get into a corresponding state of mind, or as I call it rewire your brain, and apply immediate action to it. Once you understand that, you alone create it, not the circumstances, not your past and not somebody that has told you what can and cannot be done.

Your thoughts and state of mind can make that step and after you get into the right state of mind, you can start applying the mechanics, pulling resources, finding the right people and everything else necessary to achieve your goal. Here's the secret though, just remember that you have to think beyond the present circumstances towards the desired state. Think

14

and act as you already are successful, but that doesn't mean purchase and display luxury items. It means this is a good way to train your subconscious mind so it can automate success for you just like it does automation for a lot of other tasks in your body, but we will get to this topic later.

You are the creator of your own reality and the possibilities are endless. The way technology has advanced these days, the vast amount of information at your fingertips, connectivity with the rest of the world, experts available to help you along the way, media to refer to and many other resources to tap into, you have the ultimate advantage to achieve the very results you desire.

BEND REALITY TO FIT YOUR VISION

Reality is just the way it is. Or is it?

Everything around us that is man-made has been created by the imagination and the creativity of people who refused to settle for their current reality but wanted to make it better or different. Those people are the disruptive innovators, entrepreneurs and business owners, people like you. When I was growing up as a child I always wondered why things are the way they are and who told people that's the way things should be.

Why should I sit a certain way at the desk or read a certain book I don't want to read? At music school they made me play classical music and I always played jazz and improvised. Later I became a wonderful jazz player and improviser and I still enjoy playing the music I love on my own terms.

That kind of mentality that challenges the questions "Why are things the way they are?" and "Why can't we change them?" is what made me become an entrepreneur. Even in college I wondered why the curriculum is what they tell me it should be, how do people ultimately know what it really is and how it should be.

I decided to go out on my own and become an entrepreneur and I absolutely love what I do. I get to choose who I work with, I get to choose my own team, I choose the projects to work on and I love all of my client's projects as much or even more than they do because it gives me the freedom to work freely, exercise my creativity muscle and improvise. I love using creativity during work and I encourage my team to be creative during work also. This is what creates new things and new things change the world. Different combinations of creative change by trial error process is the evolution of this universe. If your vision is strong enough, believe in it and bend the reality towards it. Don't think things have to be the way they are, but rather think about how things can be if you execute your vision.

CRACK THE CODE OF EXISTENCE

"To evolve is the meaning of life itself " -Vitaly Samonov

Animals didn't evolve simply because they didn't do anything different during their lifetime. This thought hit me after watching my cat eat and sleep all day. If you do the same thing repeatedly, you are not evolving so arguably your whole purpose of existence is defeated.

During our lifetime, the things we do, experiences we have, the way we develop our brain, things we create to better the world, things we do to evolve ourselves, other humans and the world around us is the very point of our existence as humans. If you don't do anything then no evolution is happening, in fact degradation will happen. Just like I always use the muscles at the gym reference, if you don't keep working out you will lose the muscle mass. That's what animals did for thousands of years, not much dramatically different in a creative way, and they didn't evolve in the way we did. They didn't do anything drastically new to challenge their brain. The only thing that animals did evolve are some body parts. Unlike humans, they didn't pick up a rock and start using it as an instrument to mold the environment to their advantage. That kind of drastic change is true evolution of the mind. That's why I always preach - don't copy others, create your own. That's the key to real point of progress in life, and also if you want to be vastly financially and physically rewarded

That's how our frontal lobe has evolved, as it can control your thinking process and mold you and the environment around you. The frontal lobe has awareness, rationality and many other functions that distinguish us as human beings. That's the vital part of evolution that we possess and should be evolving, not the rest of the barbaric reptilian parts of the brain. The rest of the reptilian old brain structure we have can't really be evolved, it can only be indulged though entertainment and other stimulating activities. It carries basic functionalities like eating, sleeping, fight or flight and reproducing. Some of the functionalities in the old parts of the brain we no longer need in modern society. Such as reactions and feelings like fear, fight or flight response, anger and many other survival responses. In fact, they get us in trouble and reduce modern life performance, in many social situations and during conducting business.

A PERFECT BRAIN WILL POSSIBLY CAUSE IMMORTALITY

"Who wants to live forever?" – The Queen

Life expectancy rates have dramatically increased over the past few decades as we are evolving much more rapidly now than ever before. Humans and other biological structures are vessels, that from the beginning have carried the DNA to be evolved by trial error and other natural processes. Many biological creatures have been evolving for millions of years but not until the monkey picked up some tools we started to see some rapid changes in the frontal lobe that developed into self-awareness, self-control, rationality and many other useful modern tools we use daily now.

However, we still have a large amount of reptilian brain left in the structure of our brains, which we battle daily and we are a walking ball of feelings, which really are mostly destructive and keep us from achieving ultimate performance in business and our everyday life. In recent years with the rise of technology and such vast amounts of information readily available, we are able to evolve at a much more rapid rate both biologically and in our mindset.

Nutrition, shelter and many other factors are no longer becoming an issue for the masses so creativity bursts out more and more rapidly, and we begin to thrive rather than survive. We are starting to realize that ultimately our decisions of the frontal lobe rather than reactions of the barbaric brain parts have an ultimate impact on what will happen in our lives. That's what gives us the opportunity to evolve our frontal lobe now so rapidly.

Biological vessels, or referred to as our bodies - live, eat, sleep, reproduce and die to give life to new vessels and because of experiences and decisions we made throughout our life, creatively, travel, knowledge accumulation, books we've read, human social interactions etc. we have evolved our brain and passed the new and improved DNA to new fresh vessels that can carry it on.

This process really evolves our new freshly improved version of the brain in the new vessel or so-called body. We concentrate selfishly so much on how we feel, what tastes good, how much fun we are having, what's the next thing we can selfishly indulge in, calling all this having a life. That we don't realize that those feelings exist as a guideline for us to not die from accidents, to reproduce and pass the DNA down, fight or flight response so we either fight to survive or run to survive. A lot of those if not all feelings are actually coming from our old brain structure that we no longer need in a lot of modern environment, but yet by training and indulging those old parts of the brain we keep going backwards instead of forward in evolution. That's how the masses are kept in the state of indulging and spending money by those who are aware of this and are using it to their financial and power hunger advantage. The feelings we are experiencing on a daily basis are not intended by nature for self-indulgence. They are there for guidance, but yet we continue to ignore this fact, and that is destructive behavior to our lives naturally and creates problems that you have to pay for financially and otherwise. Then we also are wondering why am I having all these problems, why my life sucks, why do I have to deal with all of this, well it's because you are paying for fun you had, a misuse of the real purpose of the brain and body. Anything in life that has brought joy and fulfilment has to be equally compensated either financially, by health or other valuables. See now why it doesn't align with the universes ultimate goal to indulge, and brings failure instead of success into life?

If we choose to make ultimately positive and carefully calculated decisions in our lives and every decision we make in our life is calculated to have best possible outcome, will we live longer, heck yes by a margin, will we evolve our DNA much more rapidly, yes, no doubt, ultimate purpose would be served. but. What does it really take to make the perfect decisions? Perfectly evolved brain. Perfect structure of the brain will possibly bring ultimate decision making, but it's up to us to evolve it to that stage by exposing it to better content, better environment and quality of life.

So if our brain didn't have to battle itself and its older parts and only had the perfect structure , our vessel or so called body will no longer need to die and reproduce because it will already have the ultimate goal accomplished to evolve the brain to the ultimate level. We would have no destructive feelings to lead us to bad behaviors and that would lead to perfection of our environment by our mind and of course perfection of the vessel that we live in. So at that point is when, I propose, immortality could be a possibility. How many biological organisms will reach immortality? Or at that point who knows at what state we will be a non-biological entity or a bio-tech hybrid. It's hard to imagine it at this point

22

of evolution, because we don't have the perfect brain currently to imagine that kind of structure yet. That kind of structure of ultimate vessel with ultimate brain could be potentially immortal as that would be the final goal of evolution. Perhaps evolution is infinite and no matter how many trillion times we increase the amount of computation and increase the quality of the environment it could be a neverending game, time will tell.

That's why - don't stress so much, accept that you are a piece of meat and just live. Will you put a dent in the universe by thriving so hard in your tiny, compared to the universe, vessel that is just one of the trillions of vessels that go through evolution? Um probably not, especially in the evolution state we are in right now which is still pretty barbaric, I mean turn on the freaking news.

So just relax, work at your own pace, enjoy life, your loved ones and don't make it all such a huge deal, your brain wants you to evolve it as rapid as possible that's why we are never satisfied but like I said before, we are not our brains we don't have to do or not do anything, we can just be.

OUR BIOLOGICAL STATE

"I'll be back" – The Terminator.

It is a fascinating question; can our biological state be replaced with technology? The answer is both yes and no. I used to think that singularity is coming shortly, but considering the biological state of the brain it might be challenging. Simply because of its ability to rewire itself, heal itself and the nimble structure of it. So, can a machine rewire itself? Its software can be self-learning, but not so much the hardware. With today's and near future technology and agile software this can be achieved, but not on the level the human body and brain can, quite yet.

Can software be built to rewire itself without outside updates of a developer? Yes, it possibly can but where will the software live - on the hardware. Hardware can't be rewired or at least not as easily as the biological brain. We will need to teach hardware to rewire itself with software to become nimble to the outside environment in order for it to become as efficient as the biological brain has been for thousands of years.

The problem though with the biological brain is there is a lot of old 'hardware' such as instincts dating back to the Stone Age that we nolonger need in today's modern society. These can be detrimental to us today. For example, the fight or flight response, fear or anger can actually end us up in deep water and they are not efficient strategies for doing business in the modern world.

So, do we still need those instincts now? Well to a certain degree yes, but I think the frontal lobe can handle fearful and emotional situations without the help of the old reptilian part of the brain because logically it can tell us how to avoid a potentially harmful situation. I believe that in the near future it will be best for us to evolve our neocortex with activities and materials that will dramatically help its evolution and we should stop feeding our brain with violence, drugs and alcohol etc.

In the future those things will disappear and no longer will be needed because it only indulges the older part of the brain, not the evolutionary part that we need to evolve. To evolve our newer parts of the brain is, I believe, the meaning of life. The brain evolves itself by feeding through knowledge and experience during our lifetime. When we reproduce, new brains emerge and start evolving, but the marks from previous generations are there. So be careful what you implement during your lifetime as it will partially pass to your future generations. So, the key is to evolve your brain as much as possible during your lifetime and pass that improved genetic to your new generation, so improved genetic codes in the brain can be passed down to each new generation afterwards. It really is our responsibility to keep on evolving, reading, creating, writing and experiencing the world to feed the brain on an evolved level.

THOUGHT IS THE MOST POWERFUL INSTRUMENT IN THE UNIVERSE

"As creators of our own reality, our thoughts create the universe around us." -Vitaly Samonov

Thought is the most powerful instrument in the universe. Try thinking about the same thing in a different way and so as you think, it will become. Our fear-based thoughts are just as powerful and attractive as positive thoughts, if not more. Science has proven that we have more negative thoughts than positive and we naturally have them so that we don't repeat bad mistakes again or harm ourselves by awaking those emotional situations that happened to us in the past. That's why we often think of bad things that happened to us long time ago and that can negatively affect who we are now and our future goals. As we label ourselves sometimes as bad people, when really it's just a reaction that happened in the crock part of our brain a long time ago. It keeps reoccurring in our minds, because the brain thinks it was a dangerous situation and is trying to protect us from it happening again. Negative thoughts were served as protection for back in the Stone Age when humans had to run away from predators and hide in caves, but now a lot of that fear is unnecessary and only is holding you back. That's why it is important to control your mind and kill negative thoughts right away before they grow out of proportion and start destroying your mind and your life. Negative thoughts can escalate and lead to numerous financial, mental and physical health issues, and they can even kill you, that happens all the time

Instead, if you choose to direct your emotions with your willpower in a positive direction then they will create miraculous things in your life financially, in business and even heal your body and health issues.

Some animals can regrow their limbs. I believe that as humans if we truly believe in it and train our brain to believe we can, then within a few generations we will be able to achieve many more seemingly impossible outcomes. While this could take thousands of years of evolution depending on how fast we can train our minds, the fact is that nobody is currently training their minds to regrow limbs so that's why we can't yet do it. Although if we become consciously aware of this through future generations and pass that new DNA down to the next generation, this could be the very key to accomplish anything and control our own evolution. We can control our own evolution with the way we think and act during our lifetime, and we really need to get out of automated evolution and into controlled by us evolution

But will it ever happen? Well it's really all up to us. If we become aware of this and get out of automatic evolution and into awareness evolution, then we can control it and accelerate the things we want to appear by training our mind. This process of mind training can really speed up and better our evolving process and get us closer to whatever the final goal of this fiasco is if there is any.

THE WAR OF OUR BARBARIC BRAINS AND OUR EVOLVED BRAINS

"Life is hard and then you die!" – many people said this.

Have you ever felt like your life is a struggle? Well it's an inner struggle between your brain parts. Our barbaric brains have been there for millions of years, and are very much so still there. For all the primitive ways of dealing with problems, life and nature has developed our brain to have fear, cold sweats, fight or flight, anger and many other unnecessary negative emotions that still occur that are no longer needed in most situations.

This is because we are not being attacked by predators or other humans in a business meeting or over the phone. The enemy is not going to kill us and take our possessions in most cases especially while conducting regular everyday tasks. Our evolved part of the brain tells us to relax but it's hard to fight all those millions of years of programming in the older part of the brain, so a lot of people just retreat into mediocracy, safety, indulgence and comfort and don't proceed with pursing their wild goals and dreams. But if you actually know what is going inside of your brain and how different parts of your brain react and interact during certain life situations, you can control it by ignoring and controlling your old parts of the brain and let the evolved parts take over and direct your beliefs and actions.

So why do we still have wars and conflicts? It is because our reptilian brain takes over when we experience fear and we react with violence instead of taking the time to think first and make a rational decision. Reaction of the old barbaric brain happens in split second, this is to save us from being eaten by the tiger or bitten by a snake, but that same thing can get us in a lot of trouble in the modern society. So, thinking before reacting is always a great idea. That type of thing happens not only in current war conflicts but in a workplace and in our everyday civilian lives. Even when people see you being successful, out of fear their un-evolved part of the brain tries to pull you down so they can stay comfortable and eliminate you as a threat. That's why your friends don't like it when you are doing better than them.

Don't listen to haters. Keep pushing forward. You can do anything, there are no limits as long as you do things legally and don't harm others, there is nothing that you cannot do, especially in first world countries. There is so much opportunity, mentorship, freedom, capital and many other resources vastly available to you. You need to tune down your old brain, engage the new brain, train it like muscles every day, feed your evolved brain useful materials like books, magazines, articles and blogs that can benefit you and increase your productivity. Don't watch indulging movies and videos on YouTube, packed with sex and violence, that does the opposite. People who show you this type of content are trying to make you vulnerable by locking you into the reptilian mindset state while they monetize on you.

Think about the future. Is what you are doing right now helping you build something positive and bigger later on or is it just short-term, immediate satisfaction seeking that is costing you money, health and time? Don't idle in the now as it leads to a life of mediocracy at best. Do something productive now with consistency to evolve your new mindset and watch as your business and lifestyle begins to evolve as a result.

EVOLVING THE BRAIN THROUGH READING

"We are what we mentally eat!"

I love reading, in fact I am addicted to it. If I want to learn about something that I want to accomplish in life in the most efficient way possible, I read about it and this provides me with building blocks to be prepared for the task. I owe a lot of success in my life personally and in business to reading and expanding my knowledge base and mindset horizons. Through books we are able to learn from experts that have gone though trial error process and years, sometimes a lifetime, of research and knowledge accumulation before us on the subject we are reading about and have the information packaged into an easy to follow instruction manual.

My favorite topics are psychology, neuroscience, human behavior, philosophy, self-improvement, success, motivation, and of course business. I think that having a balanced life, healthy mind, body, relationships and spiritual awareness are crucial for success financially and in business. It's like a wheel, if it's not well rounded and has a chip in it the wheel then will not go fast. It will have to stop for frequent repairs, and that creates stress and frustration and takes away from the focus and dedication you need to give to your business and personal life.

OUR ANCESTORS DIDN'T FIGHT FOR OUR FREEDOM IN VAIN

"War, what is it good for, absolutely nothing." - Edwin Starr

Our ancestors didn't go to wars to fight for our freedom for you to sit back, waste time and indulge in meaningless activities like sitting in front of TV eating chips or sitting at a bar wasting time and money watching a game. These things are great in moderation to relax but not if it becomes an obsession and an addiction. If you become obsessed with indulging, that becomes your life and you become good at it. As you practice it over and over again, like an athlete practicing a move for the Olympics, only you are a couch athlete or a bar athlete. As social human beings, it's nice to reward yourself and indulge occasionally it actually increases performance and motivates you. However, you must be focused on the right things.

I know this from personal experience because I used to indulge too much on the social side in college and it became destructive behavior for me until I started to obsess with the things I really wanted in life like finding meaningful work, making a change for the better and making other people happy and motivated by my work. That's what truly made me happy. I feel like indulging can make you depressed because you know you are not making an impact and not progressing but rather just chasing the next short-term satisfaction. Although we seek comfort and to indulge in life, it has to be paid for financially and with health. Comfort and indulgence gets punished by nature, because we are supposed to be evolving not going backward in evolution of our brain and our body.

You will not find happiness when you are only indulging your reptilian part of the brain because the brain is naturally programmed to strive to evolve. The art of evolving and moving forward is the key to creating true happiness as opposed to sideways progressions. Such as socializing, using alcohol, food and drugs to intensify the amount of endorphins released by your brain so you can feel good for the moment. Then have to pay for it later with health, finances and broken relationships. A large part of our brain craves these endorphin releasing activities but you have to suppress it with your rational part of the brain and delay gratification in order to create a sustainable life of real happiness. Not a temporary bandage that covers the wound instead of giving it the proper treatment.

I believe we are currently existing during the part of evolution when it's very difficult for us to balance the old and new way of thinking and parts of the brain from different eras of evolution, because they want different things. So, the challenge is to balance your mind enough that you don't get deprived in either part of the brain. Giving emphasis and more training to the more evolved parts of the brain, like the neocortex. If you are to be obsessed with something in life make sure it is a healthy obsession and helps you go forward. Growing is the key, as it matches natures requirements for any live organism.

For instance, in order to create a billion-dollar business, you have to become pretty obsessed about it. However, if your other parts of the brain and body, the ones that aren't working on the creation of the business, are really deprived in a negative way then you will end up with depression, anxiety, health problems, broken relationships and resentment. I personally dedicate about 80 percent of my brainpower to activities I am after, such as work, and 20% I am using to ensure my mind is balanced with health, relationships, socializing etc., which does also increase performance for the other 80% part of my life dramatically.

Different strategies work differently for different people as we have been exposed to different environments, experiences and influences in our lives. In general, we all have the same brain structure so by knowing how the brain is structured and catering to those brain parts has really worked for me in my life. That's why I love reading about neuroscience and I highly recommend investing some time into this topic for you as well.

IT'S NEVER TOO DIFFICULT

"Difficulties are like weights at the gym, they make us grow." – Vitaly Samonov

The mindset for extreme success is never to put any barriers or limits on your mind and your actions. Always analyze if what you are thinking or saying is negative or if it is a stopping belief in any way from what you are trying to achieve, and you will be surprised. In fact, the bolder you are with your actions and your words, the more you will succeed on a higher level, because the only person that can really stop you from achieving what you want, is you. The untrained mindset is like a flee in a can - if it is conditioned to jump only to the lid that's closed, once the lid is open it will not jump higher than that. However, we are not fleas, we have a highly-sophisticated brain structure that we can easily tap into. That allows us to realize situations with rationality and self-awareness and make the decision to jump as high as we want.

So why do we fear so much what other people think? It's all in your mind. Once you get older you realize that nobody's opinion ever really mattered and that the chances are that they never really cared that much in the first place. You think people around you are thinking and taking about you, but they really don't as much as you think. That is why it is so important to always do what's right for you.

If you think something is too difficult for you, it will be. If you think that thing that you desire to have or accomplish so much is too hard or unattainable, you will not accomplish it. You have limited yourself before you have even started. If you start taking action to achieve the things that you thought were too difficult, you will see that it's actually achievable. For example, it's not that difficult to do well financially if you save, invest right and exercise self-discipline. You can do very well financially with any level of income. The only thing that is stopping you is your lack of self-education on that subject followed by executing proper actions, and being afraid of failure during the trial error process. I always wonder why so many people want to do well financially or so called be rich, and they don't educate themselves on that topic.

It is important to have the self-discipline to not execute things that could jeopardize your goal. It doesn't require advanced calculus or even an advanced degree to do well financially especially in the modern world. If you want a beautiful home in a nice neighborhood then evaluate your current financial position. Do some simple math to see how much savings and proper investment it will take for you to get there and execute it.

If this cannot be accomplished with your current business or job and the goal is so important to you, then switch to doing business in a way that will generate the actual income that aligns mathematically to accomplish your goal. The ability to achieve your dreams is in your hands. Regardless of whether you desire to travel, help those less fortunate around the globe, start your own business, achieve financial freedom or create a freedom-based lifestyle that will allow you to spend more time with your family - do it now. Life is too short, get out of your own way and go for it.

PART

2

BUSINESS SUCCESS

THE SECRET TO LANDING BIG CLIENTS

The challenge with business is people.

The clients who are low budget and have not conducted business in the past are often emotional and unstable, they have to be guided along the way and are always on the edge of thinking that they are being ripped off or if things are not perfect then it's somebody else's fault, that's why they fail at their business and honestly nobody can help them for any money if they can't help themselves. They didn't build the experience of working with others yet and give up at the first sign of difficulty, if they are just starting out, have no budget and they also think that others will simply just do all the work for them while they sit back and get all the results, and they don't know how to and don't want to put efforts into their own projects, and only expect perfect results from others and not themselves.

The big budget clients are often the people who already have created the budget to begin with, so they had to conduct business in the past in order to earn the money, there for they are more emotionally intelligent in business and are able to stick with the process, be patient during any setbacks, have good understanding of the requirements of the tasks, are pleasure to work with and are flexible with the process as a whole. They are harder to come by, but it's better to have a few of these quality clients than to have a bunch of small ones who drain all of your energy and end up unsatisfied regardless of what you do, those petty clients are the people who are not successful from the inside so the business they will conduct on the outside is not going to be either.

The big client is going to also see if you are a bozo firm or an individual to work with as they have experience and they see how you conduct business usually from the very first meeting, so know and demonstrate your value in order to get valuable clients, that is the not so secret. And one of the first things is if you are showing low value of your firm or your service, by setting a low price point and attracting bozo clients, then you are scrapping to try to make ends meet. So, my advice is: take the time to learn your client and their personality, before you get into the process with them as your work can be heaven or hell, depending on the people you work with.

HOW TO ACTUALLY DO IT, REAL FACTUAL INFORMATION ZERO HYPE

A lot of people are seeking how to start a business, how to be your own boss, how to make money online, a lot of information is flying around, a lot of luring marketing technics without actual factual information on how to do it and what to do. How do you become rich doing it yourself, how do you make income online or from home or from your office or any other place you want to be may be like Thailand or a private Island or from a tent on the beach, everyone is trying to figure things out and everyone is always asking these questions everywhere, so why is nobody really giving factual information out, well you have to invest time and money bottom line, invest time to train your mind first, invest in real books and pay for them don't just read free pamphlets created for single purpose to create marketing hype and lure people in. Then implement your knowledge and research, or you can just do it first and then learn from the trial error process yourself, regardless trial error will be involved in your work, by doing it you will find out how to do it. So here is what to do if you want real business not pyramid scam and not teaching people to teach people to teach people, never-ending teaching with no real action, a lot of this is going on right now. Here is how I and my team actually do it.

Look at what people need to solve, a need or a problem, then brainstorm ideas and combine them, research if that exists and it probably already does, no worries, twist it a bit and make it unique, like a cell phone cover or a shower head, or a drone or an app in a different way, it has to be better or different than current product to solve some current need, if it already exists, good that means there is demand for it and people are buying it, make it unique and more attractive than what exists, this has to come from your mind, from you and be original, create it don't copy things exactly, that will put you at a disadvantage on the marketplace. Then find investors, I would say ten thousand bucks Is enough to get almost any project going, you can do fundraising, you can find private or other investors. Investing yourself or family money is the best way as you are not dependent on anyone else. Then hire a team, you can outsource any work or get a local team it's up to you, outsourcing is challenging because it takes a while to find legitimate workers and not scam artists who grab money and deliver 10% effort. Then after your team is solid implement your idea and launch it as fast as possible, go live and test if people want it, collect feedback from people and see if it picks up, if it's a membership project see if people sign up, if it's a physical product see if people buy and what kind of feedback they give, listen to feedback and that will give you further ideas on how to change, evolve and improve your project. After that you have to pick up traction or abandon or keep twisting it to a point where it does pick up traction. Once it picks up traction and say you have thousands of active users using your product you can either put further budget into the project to grow it finding other investors and you can grow it into the next Facebook, or you can just sell it out on the auction or to an interested investor who can grow it further while keeping a percentage of that company so that if later it becomes the next Facebook then you own a stock.

After you sell you can take that money and invest into the next idea and at that point you are more experienced and your mind will automatically know what to do and what marketing strategy works best for that type of product and you will implement it a lot easier. Projects can be anything, a book to give you credibility as a consultant or a gadget that solves peoples need, or a software that also solves people's needs and provides optimization of their time and money for them. If you have many active users, your product is valuable and it can run on itself without your supervision, that means you can sell it to someone else who can run it from there, but if the project completely depends on you then it's tougher to sell, you might find investors to invest into your team to keep working on it because it is dependent on your team and you can grow it and yourself in value while paying yourself a salary from a portion of the investments. I touch base on this strategy later on in the book as well.

Another way to do business is the very obvious – to provide service but it's not the way to make millions upon millions while you sleep, provide real service. Think what you are an expert in and start providing that expertise to others and charge money. If you want to up your skill, then keep practicing and learning it more. Then you can get clients and do it for them or teach them to do it. You can provide real information on how to do it, or you can do it for them and charge money. So, if somebody needs something done you simply charge them for it, or you teach them how to do it and you get compensated, this is really just a no brainer. You can open your own firm, brand it, hire people and start doing projects and provide service for other people, this is actual work and you have to do it with maximum integrity and provide maximum value in order to get compensated vastly.

If you train yourself and brand yourself to be THE expert in the field you can charge more and people will pay, because of your reputation of prior work and/or the marketing reputation you put into yourself or your firm. You can also scale this model by hiring more people, opening new locations, getting investors involved and putting more money into marketing, branding and training the skills for yourself and your team. After you make actual money with actual product or service you can play around with stock market portfolios, real estate, become an investor and seek out talented teams who already have good traction and help them get to the next level financially and any other investment you want to preserve, invest or gamble your money with. This pretty much sums it up if you want to make real money with real business and provide real value. Don't waste your time on scams and bozo experts, do the real deal.

LEARNING FROM FAILURE

"Success is stumbling from failure to failure with no loss of enthusiasm."
- Winston Churchill

Even if you think you have failed, you really haven't. You just have to adjust your strategy or recognize your errors and correct them. The key is to break out of the mindset of impossibility and not let past failures hold you back. If a business or a person is already doing what it is you are striving to achieve, then it means it can be done and you can train yourself to do it just as well as they did.

If you are a so called 'Solopreneur,' you will not always have the knowledge, time, skills or training to do everything yourself, so you can hire or outsource people to do the task just like the other company or individual does it. It's all about having the right people on board, or as I like to say it - the right people on the bus. If somebody is not performing and you are not getting the result you need to get, it's not that they are a bad person or are unskilled, they may just not be the best fit for this particular role in your company or your company's culture and will perform better elsewhere. If this happens, you need to replace them in order to let your business continue to grow and succeed.

Some would say that failure just means you need to work harder and to not let it stop you from achieving your dreams. But I believe that it's more of a trial and error process and this actually is an effective process in business, especially for startups. When you try first and then adjust the strategy accordingly after it doesn't particularly work out to your advantage, there is no failure in that, it's just a part of the strategy to get the result that you desire. Of course, coming in being a bit more prepared and taking more calculated risks is crucial, because then it will eliminate wasted time, financial costs, stress and reduce work hours to achieve the results you are after. That's why reading books, doing market research and learning from mentors is crucial before embarking on a business adventure.

When it comes to risks, particular in startups, take only calculated risks with as minimum risk as possible, and have a fallback plan, when you are first starting, you don't know what you are doing yet and you need to be able to be prepared financially and otherwise to give it a second shot after adjusting your strategy when you fail the first time. In fact, if you can have a backup plan, always do, so you can minimize your losses in the end. That is why I do not recommend getting a loan when you start up a business, especially if it is your first time and you don't really have the experience or knowledge of what you are doing yet. Your first idea will often fail and your second idea is born out of it. At this point you are more experienced and you will succeed better and faster, but you still have to repay the money back for the first idea, if you went with the borrowing money route. I recommend trying to find sponsorship elsewhere, in the family or offer equity, find investors interested in your idea, niche and or your team, but I don't recommend getting a loan with a payback percentage attached to it.

Did you know that it took over ten thousand unsuccessful attempts to invent the light bulb? I am sure that during each failure, it was taken into consideration what needs to be improved or not done again in order to find the right way for it to work. So, the point is to keep trying, just don't get in debt and make sure you have a bullet proof back up plan.

My own experience with failure is that if I don't give something enough focus and do a mediocre job it will not work. Remember that many others are trying to do it as well and you have to sharpen your strategy to make yours better or different. Pay attention to details, as small things create synergy between each other and can push what you are doing to the next level exponentially.

Care about what you do. Truly care. This approach has always worked for me. Don't rely on work half done and ask yourself why it's not working. You must be a hundred percent committed and continuously improve the way you implement business. Why for instance clients can't find you?

What is something small you can improve at this point to make it easier for them to find you? If you're not on the first page of Google for example, get on it. First page Google ranked results get on average five times more traffic. Always put yourself in the shoes of your customers and ask yourself what they want. Your clients are smart, they research, they learn. Always ask for feedback - that can give you credibility and create online business presence and awareness, hire a blogger, do social networking to build an organic community of followers for your brand, who will be eager to purchase anytime you have something new and exciting to offer. So, strive for integrity to shine through on the level that potential prospects for your business will see and feel, that will separate you from competition in any business niche.

Here are a few of the most common (and avoidable) causes of failure in business and otherwise:

- Poorly defined goals

- Lack of ambition or determination (not giving it a hundred percent)

- Lack of education about what you are doing. Self-made educators receive the best kind of education. You have a zone of genius so stick to it and get others to help you with the rest. Don't try and do it all yourself

- Lack of self-discipline

- Lack of mind-body health (i.e. not exercising, eating poorly, negative thoughts)

- Procrastination

- Lack of persistence (good starters are not necessarily good finishers)

- Negative mindset and personality (this will make it difficult for anyone to want to work for or with you)

- Over cautiousness (taking no chances or calculated risks)

- Wrong selection of team mates in business (get the right people on the bus)

- Lack of focus

- Overspending and overindulging

- Egotism and arrogance

- Guessing instead of thinking (you must acquire the facts on which to think accurately instead of relying on opinions)

- Personal life problems (relationships, problems with the law, financial, spirituality)

- Perfectionism (never get started)

SURVIVING VS. THRIVING

"The best part of life is not just surviving, but thriving with passion and compassion and humor and style and generosity and kindness." -Maya Angelou

In order to thrive you need to first survive. If your survival needs are not met and you are at a risk of homelessness and starvation, then there is no possible way you could strive in your endeavor of choice. Once you have a nice cushion financially and otherwise to work on the endeavor you are after then you can truly thrive because you don't have to worry about the finances and you have a piece of mind and security that tomorrow there will be bread on your table. In order to survive first, you have to manage your budget to a point where you produce a lot more than you spend and save enough cushion for you to be able to roll over into a thriving zone where money is working for you and you are starting to thrive at what you want and love to do with passion and enthusiasm, knowing that you have rain boots locked and loaded for when that day comes. So, don't lease a fully loaded BMW on a salary that is less than the car is, and when economy goes bad you get laid off or your clients don't have any money to pay you, or there are no clients. Purchase the rainy-day shoes, aka invest your money into assets that will generate income so you don't have to worry and work on the projects of your dreams, doesn't that sound great. Well lots of people shoot for that immediate satisfaction in their crock brain when they see the Beemer and shell out the big bucks, it's ok if you can sustain it, I personally don't buy anything unless it's like buying a candy bar or a safety pin and doesn't bust your budget, so If it is going to affect your overall balance sheet, don't do it go for the rainy-day shoes, because that's what will allow you to work on and sustain your dreams during the more challenging seasons of life.

EXPECTATIONS VS. APPRECIATION

"The human nature is – it's never enough."

It is a good practice to set your standards and expectations high as that alone will determine the level of your life right now and in the future. However, in order to gain any kind of fulfillment, true appreciation of what you already have and have accomplished must be achieved first.

Without appreciation, it seems like a never-ending game that leaves people angry and frustrated, it is easy for people stepping into the next level to think that everyone around them are smarter, more fortunate or possess more things or experiences than they do. In this obscure perception, they neglect to recognize how far they have come and how much they already have achieved.

There will always be somebody that has more than you; more athletic abilities, more education, more experience or any other factor you want to compare yourself to. However, in reality, if you are satisfied at your current level and have a great amount of confidence while still striving to achieve more, it will bring way more fulfillment than the endless chase or competition. Combining gratitude for what you have

57

now, while striving to achieve more, I believe is a great combination for happiness and overall wellness.

DISCIPLINE AND FOCUS IN BUSINESS

The best way to stay disciplined and focused in business is to set a Wildly Important Goal (WIG).

Focusing on your WIG is never automatic it takes effort. You set WIGS to direct energy and concentration for yourself and the team and work to accomplish the most important goal. It will also give you clarity on the areas that you can conserve energy on elsewhere.

If you create focus for your team you can truly accomplish extraordinary goals. I recommend setting no more than one or two WIGs per team at any one time. Like any goal, a WIG has to be structured with a clear start and end date with key deadlines, outcomes and milestones.

MARKETING 101

Sales is king. It is a fact that most start-ups fail because of lack of the proper marketing. Business is twenty percent product, content or service and eighty percent marketing. Not implementing marketing is like winking in the dark, you know you did it but nobody else saw.

You are one of the best people who can market yourself and your business, simply because you care about its success more than anyone else. You can train yourself just like any other professional marketer did. Today there are so many resources available online such as YouTube videos, Mentors, e-books etc. to train yourself.

However, this is not to say don't involve marketing professionals and learn from them when you can, especially if you have the budget. In which case I recommend hiring somebody smarter than you in that field so you can learn from them. At the same time, you can up-skill yourself as well and save yourself valuable time, while they are doing the work for you so you can concentrate on sticking to your 'zone of genius' or area of expertise. At the end of the day, what is more valuable than marketing and getting your product and service out there? Some people even manage to market nothingness so good that people will buy it, like pyramid scams and many other affiliate marketing things. This is not to say all affiliate marketing is a scam.

I suggest learning the basics of marketing and doing it yourself while all other technical tasks can be done by hiring proper experts and employees. Marketing is one of the most important factors in your product or service. If you have a great product or service, without other people knowing about it you would not be able to sell it. There are many books about marketing and I highly recommend reading some of the timeless classics as well as new books to get the insights. I am not going to list an endless list of recommendations here, just do a little research and read the ones that appear most suitable for your business. While the marketing space is constantly evolving at a rapid rate a lot of the core marketing methods stay the same.

Marketing changes very rapidly and competitors are trying to innovate as fast as possible to get to the clients first. If you are not doing it than you risk losing clients to your competition. Start marketing and selling now if you want to succeed at all.

One tip of advice I would make is: always try to be useful instead of amazing. Start really caring about giving value and making the difference with your product, content or service and not just chasing a quick buck with a quick hype. That will never give you the steady flow of trustworthy clients, and build a professional network of people who you can rely on during financial crisis. Be there for your clients and give as much as you can for free. Yes, you heard correctly, go overboard with how much value you really give. That will also separate you from the competition. Offer a lot of extra things to customers that are extras and free, in most cases a customer will not go that far anyways, but it will give you an advantage to provide more options over your competition. So, overpromise and over deliver.

Once true trust is built you will be surprised by how fast people's loyalty is gained and lifelong clients are created who keep on referring new ones and leaving the good feedback. Long term trust is factual and not packed with artificial hype. By helping someone out today with useful information, services or products, it will return to you in equal or multiplied reward. The more people you provide value to, the greater the payback is.

There are many different marketing strategies for each kind

of business. For instance, a local business may want to advertise on local Facebook pages and set up Facebook campaigns to target local clients they you want to reach. They may also want to create videos and post them on YouTube and other social media platforms. Cash is king, yes during the industrial age and before that it was and maybe it still is, but with the rise of the connected age there is a new sheriff in town – content, and it is important to create fresh, bold, engaging, consistent and creative content on a regular basis, to keep your current clients and prospects engaged and aware of your product and service.

Ranking highly on the web with a front-page position is important, particularly through relevant keywords on Google locally, as that gives your business credibility automatically.

Reliable resources such as high-ranking PR blogs can provide you with credibility, so can reviews, references and publicity generated from celebrities or influencers with a following promoting your brand.

Global marketing campaigns require a higher budget and are more abstract. That is why I suggest starting your marketing efforts locally and more targeted, especially for startups. As mentioned, you will need to create content consistently. That will grab peoples' interest and gain familiarity with your brand. Consistency is a key factor in marketing by converting prospects into fans and fans into customers for life.

OVER CONTENT EXPOSURE CREATES ANXIETY AND STRESS

"Don't feed your brain any negative content if you want to get ahead in life." – Vitaly Samonov

One of the main reasons why people have such high anxiety, anger, which is also fear, and stress levels now these days is due to the amount of garbage content they are being bombarded with on a daily basis. You can't go anywhere without a brand attacking people to purchase their product and competing for our attention. And a lot of it is not even a brand, mostly some kind of luring attention grabbing bizarre stunts and news hijacking, desperately trying to grab attention from masses and it works, like all the obviously staged and fake, existing purely for traffic purposes videos on YouTube of pranks, homeless people, cute cats etc. If we learn to switch off from social media at least for a while, we don't have to deal with that anymore and free our life and brain for bettering ourselves, create our own agenda, and create more real quality time with loved ones instead. Because what is mostly waiting for you on your phone is someone else's agenda, and then do you have time left for your own?

Taking a strategic thinking approach involves relearning how you think about the world. It just takes time to learn and practice. Don't get stuck with the same way of thinking for too long because the world around you is constantly changing, reinvent yourself to meet ever evolving market needs.

What you believe and value controls your destiny and it continuously changes during different stages of your life. When you are consuming content it is often brainwashing you, mostly subconsciously, to get the desired emotional triggers so you can purchase the product subliminally or in your face during that content exposure. If you are consuming content that is relative to your goals or values, it will align your brain and thoughts in the direction of your goal. With so much information around us constantly attacking and competing for our attention, it is important to consume only content that is beneficial to your goal and keep reading or watching it as it will help you train your brain like a muscle, so you can lift bigger problems out of your way to the top.

If your own a business, don't look and copy at what others

do, that's not creativity. Animals are not creative, that's why they didn't evolve their neocortex the way we did. Monkey see monkey do. Do your own thing, that will distinguish you from the rest. You and your creativity and the way of thinking is the unique business niche you have been looking for. A unique or distinctive product, content or service will always trump the copy cats. Offering practical value helps make things catch on and using storytelling to convey information is really important. Build real credibility not fake hype, as people are very skeptical these days with the amount that they are being marketed to.

FORMING SUCCESSFUL HABITS AND STRATEGIES IN BUSINESS AND LIFE

"We are what we repeatedly do. Excellence, then, is not an act, but a habit." – Aristotle

If you want to be successful, you need to stop consuming non-valuable information that takes up your most precious resource – your time. Instead use the time to create content and / or your product or service. If you want to earn serious money and be successful in your business, you have to learn to create and not just consume.

If you want to earn more income, than plan for the future by frugally investing the time you have now into something that will produce income for you later. Time is a resource that if utilized and leveraged correctly will produce profits without you trading time for money (otherwise known as the concept of residual income). For example, you can create an all-weather portfolio of stocks and bonds that will generate enough income for you to be financially free and not have to work. It works the same way in business whereby if you spend a lot of money on luxurious items while you are in the start-up phase, this will take away the time and energy that could have been invested frugally into the work and progress of your business instead.

In business, being frugal is not only important with money but even more so with time. Spend your time wisely and your chances of success will increase. It is simply a matter of dedicating and focusing your energy. Everything takes energy from a routine task like going grocery shopping to worrying about the bills.

The key to generating successful habits is to understand your WHY. Why are you doing this? Why is this important to you? If you have a strong WHY it will create momentum for the work you are doing and move you forward faster.

Making effective decisions (based on your WHY) is ultimately what is going to determine your course of destiny in your career, business and other aspects of life. As I always preach, well-informed and sensible decisions will almost always lead to great results. Keeping your WHY in mind will help guide you through some tough decisions. When it comes to making effective decisions, chance and luck have very little to do with it. So, calculate, research, gather reliable resources, create a back-up plan and set realistic (but optimistic) goals.

Taking action is the final vital step in actually making it all happen. Make consistent action a habit. Business is always evolving and you will need to adjust your strategy during the process and innovate as fast as possible. It helps to constantly research, learn from the experts and train your brain through repetition.

For example, repetition is how musical instruments are learned and how athletes train their bodies. If people are exposed to something long enough they will eventually start to learn or be persuaded. This strategy is proven in marketing and works by tapping into your brain on a subconscious level.

The subconscious mind is very powerful and is where our

habits are formed, both good and bad. When you have a clear and properly trained by repetition of positive tasks subconscious mind, you will have no limits as to what you can accomplish. Our subconscious mind however also controls our conscience. Sometimes if our conscious says something, it is speaking from the subconscious mind and the habits that we have developed there. It will tell us to do something that we are supposed to do, even if it is not the best solution for what we are trying to accomplish.

That's why be aware of this and stop negative automated in the subconscious mind tasks. You can simply tell yourself, this is just a bad habit that I can unwire from my mind with overcoming it with willpower a few times, and replacing it with other positive automated habits.

The way to 'un-train' your subconscious mind is by overpowering it with our conscious mind repeatedly to make it aware of how you want things to be. Some people use hypnosis but if you understand the concept of how your subconscious mind works then you can train your subconscious mind yourself and you will accomplish what you consciously want. I firmly believe that this alone will bring happiness, prosperity and joy into your life, relationships and business because your expectations will

68

align with the situation that you've create as well as experiencing the satisfaction of your accomplishments.

OPTIMIZE YOUR PERFORMANCE

"World domination is such an ugly phrase. I prefer to call it world optimization." - Eliezer Yudkowsky

I strive to optimize everything in my life so it runs on automation and I can keep focused on my WIG (Wildly Important Goal) such as a certain big project I may be working on. I recommend that if you are trying to become successful at your WIG, you need to look at all aspects of your life and think about what is really slowing you down. Is your home or your dwelling a tool to live in or is it draining all of your time, energy and budget? Is your body healthy or is it in a less desirable state and is constantly causing you to feel less than your best? Are your relationships with people not ultimately blissful, and more of a rocky road ice-cream flavor?

Take athletes for example. Some go to extreme lengths to trim any excess fat on their bodies and diet, literally wiping the fat of the cottage cheese and other foods in order to optimize their performance. Just a split second of improvement to their performance could lead to breaking a new record. Similarly, many small factors of your life that you don't even realize, really do affect your performance, like an athlete's diet, by simply eliminating some components in your life that drag you down, you will be surprised at the results you can achieve. I always look to optimize my time. For instance, while I am making a tea, I am throwing in laundry and reading a book. Time is one of the most important assets we have and when optimized properly, wonderful things start happening in our lives.

There are many modern tools that can help you optimize your performance in your business and personal life. One of my and my team's current projects is a highly customizable platform for the next generation of business, freelancers and entrepreneurs that will optimize your time and performance, response rate and social aspects to build valuable relationships and networks. It's a very beginner friendly platform that involves organizing workflow, compacting and displaying data, and displaying opportunities and pitfalls to give you better control of your life and business and put you back in the driver's seat. We are also currently working on a unique and fun social messaging platform packed with unique features and that involves some other exciting projects.

Remember, your competition in your field is always optimizing their business and constantly looking for ways to improve to get ahead. Always look for tools like automation and optimization software and implement it into your daily life and business. This kind of tools will definitely put you head and shoulders above any competition in your niche.

It is important to optimize your time when your brain is in the most creative state. When an idea strikes, you write it down, don't wait but take immediate action. Or when epiphany strikes, you quickly write it down, as the chances are you will forget what brought you to that 'aha' moment.

Don't force your brain to be creative when it isn't, as the time spent on unfocused or sloppy work could have been spent on relaxing and recharging or any activity that can lead to more time for your brain to be in the peak state. Peak performance should be used on your most important tasks. Physical stimulation really affects the brain. Being smart is a relative term and it depends on a sum of practices and time spent on evolving your mind with useful materials in the area that you want to be an expert in. Being smart is really being smart in an area or a number of areas of expertise as you can't be an expert in everything.

PROVIDE VALUE

"It is no use saying "we are doing our best." You have to succeed in doing what is necessary." – Winston Churchill

I am obsessed and committed to providing genuine value to people when I am working or just interacting with them and I truly care about their success, that's what made me successful at what I do, really, it's my niche I would say. I feel like a quick buck is good only for a while, but to build lasting relationships for business and in personal life, you have to truly go all out and provide more value than others can, do extra, give extra, go the extra mile. I base my relationships with people in my life, my team and clients on total trust and understanding of the goals we are trying to achieve and I know that the final results matters, it doesn't matter that we have tried and did something, we have to achieve what we have envisioned, without the final result process can teach you things but it will not provide the results that people really pictured to have. To take clients vision and really mold it into a real product, really is a blissful process for me. I enjoy to see other people happy because of me and my and my teams work, that's what motivates me. And I would recommend this strategy to anyone conducting business and for everyday human interaction. Be that guy who cares, and watch the quality of your relationships, network and friendships skyrocket.

LEADERS ARE READERS

"Not all readers are leaders, but all leaders are readers." – Harry S. Truman

If you want to be a great leader, you need to feed your brain. One of the best ways to do this is by reading books. Audible books are my favorite as it allows you to multitask while listening. I used to listen to tapes by Tony Robbins back in the day. And he said that he really had this passion and hunger to find out how things really work, how to make more money and find more meaning in life. He said that he has read nearly 700 books on these topics and it hit me right then. If he succeeded on such an enormous level then this tactic really works. And I was right, as soon as I started reading around a hundred books a year my life drastically changed in every way especially in business, every type of success including financial started knocking on my door, I eliminated many of my personal insecurities, I literally used a book branded anti-skeleton closet spray, I now understand how the world and peoples' minds work better, I became a better communicator, can better handle any situations and surrounding in my everyday life, by reading and applying the knowledge blocks I have accumulated from reading, and a lot of it came automatically, as I so to say was brainwashing myself with good materials and they started to appear in my life and my actions started to reflect. To apply the knowledge is more important than just to acquire it, especially to apply it creatively, having knowledge is like sitting in a Ferrari and not pressing the gas. But in many books, it tells you to apply the knowledge, and it sinks in your subconscious mind and becomes a real habit, so you go and start automatically implementing all the good things you have exposed yourself to in the books, it's like magic. Knowledge is power. But again, just reading books isn't going to get you where you need to be. You need to apply the knowledge to reality.

Don't just keep doing the same thing without innovating as that's how you get stuck with it for the rest of your life and that's who you become – you become what you do, and if in the future you get killed by the innovators in that niche then you got nothing. But if you keep innovating and growing then that will be your key. Same goes for - don't work with the same people if they don't perform exactly how you want, hire others, work with other teams and try people out, there are millions of experts in the world and some of them are so talented that they alone will pick up your business, idea or even your life.

WHY DO SOME SUCCEED WHILE OTHERS FAIL?

"Try not to become a man of success. Rather become a man of value." - Albert Einstein

So why do some succeed and others fail, the truth is that there are many reasons for this, some offer a better product or service or a better price point. Some provide more value to people and businesses and some have better marketing or both.

It is important when wanting your business or endeavor to succeed that you're not just in it for the monetary gains or self-indulging goals. When you are focused on delivering value through your product or service, that's what is going to bring (sustained) success. Of course, this needs to have an excellent marketing and sales strategy implemented.

But this is not always the case. Sometimes even given the same set of circumstances it is hard to determine why one became more successful than the other however a key determinant is social interaction. Word of mouth is incredibly important to your business. People will always trust another personal recommendation. Taking advantage of this in your business is the key to its success. I believe that virality isn't born but rather created and that when someone figures out how to make something to be talked about, then they will start to see real success.

EMOTIVE APPEAL

"Products are created in the factory, but brands are created in the mind"
- Walter Landor

To make your product popular, it is important to show visible subjects of status or social currency to show others that 'importance', 'coolness' or any other positive status can be achieved by associating themselves with your product. Everyone wants to appear 'cool' and when these associations are attached to a particular product, service or content they will trigger emotions that get passed on virally.

Content needs to be useful in order to go viral. Engrave your product or message into stories that people want to pass on. Word of mouth is used to achieve desirable social impressions. Find your product's inner remarkability that will catch on quickly to your audience and promote this angle. People don't just care how they are doing themselves but more so in comparison with others, like getting the latest gadgets before everyone else.

Don't just keep doing the same thing without innovating as that is how you get stuck with it for the rest of your life. You become what you repeat. If you don't keep up with changes in the market, what your customers' needs are and what your competitors are doing, you will find yourself out of business. But if you keep innovating and growing, you will secure your place on the market. When it comes to innovation, speed beats perfection in most cases, so innovate fast enough for your clients to stay interested in your product.

Commercials and ads trigger you to act just like certain surroundings trigger you to act a certain way such as behaving differently in church as you would in at a fine dining restaurant or at work. With this in mind it can be used to your business advantage. For instance, people at a fine dining restaurant would be psychologically more prepared to spend and tip way more money than in less nice surroundings. Sometimes even bad reviews can trigger sales as long as it reminds people that the product exists.

When we care, we share! Good experiences with products or services causes us to share relevant articles and like posts or videos on social media. We also like highly emotive stories, the real-life struggles or 'zero to hero' scenarios. Emotion sells and triggers a better response because most people already know the information about a product or service but they don't always act and they need a further trigger.

When you are consuming content, it's brainwashing you to consume more of it and spread it like wildfire to others. If you are consuming content that is relative to your goal it will align your brain and thoughts in the right direction and you will accomplish your goal faster. Be careful to only consume content that is beneficial to you and your goals. Subscribe to content relative to your goal and keep reading, watching and learning. It will help you think straight while working on your accomplishments. Others are likely to imitate what everyone else around them is doing. Don't follow what others do just because it's popular or it's the way it is. Consumers are so caught up on getting a good deal that they are sometimes getting caught up in paying more instead.

Don't focus on what others are doing. Do your own thing that will distinguish you from others, but don't forget this is different than trying to learn how the successful people did it. Don't reinvent the wheel. Offering practical and valuable information helps make ideas and concepts catch on. Use stories as vessels because if the information is made more interesting it's more likely to get passed alone

In relationships when you think the other person has changed and you don't want to be with them anymore ask yourself if tthings really have changed or the way you look at things changed because generally speaking every seven to ten years, people change their values and beliefs and that triggers divorces. Media shapes perceptions but have your own opinion. Don't give up what you want most for what you want now.

In business, when you prove to yourself that what you are doing works then you just need to focus on leveraging and scaling it. If you are doing something that has no probability of making you achieve that goal, then stop doing it. The subconscious mind is more powerful than your conscious mind and if you can influence it then you can change almost anything in your life.

There is so much noise today, particularly on social media so you have to really shock people with your content. Content that is shocking gets passed alone and sparks conversation. Differences of opinions spark debate that attracts a lot of people and gives viral boost to your content.

PRICE ANCHORING

As the saying goes, the best way to sell a $600 watch is to put it right next to a $20000 watch. This is because of a common cognitive bias called Anchoring. Anchoring refers to the tendency to heavily rely on the first piece of information offered when making a decision.

WEBER'S LAW

According to a principle known as Weber's Law, the noticeable difference between two stimuli is directly proportional to the magnitude of the stimuli. In other words, making a change to something is affected by how big that thing was before, for example, price increases for products and services. When it comes to price increases, Weber's Law proves that approximately ten percent is the average point where customers will respond. Of course, there are many variables that affect a price increase but this law presents an accurate rule of thumb for determining price points.

YOU CAN BE, DO OR HAVE ANYTHING YOU WANT

"Liberate yourself from what you 'should' be doing" – Vitaly Samonov

From the early age we have been brainwashed by Hollywood movies, celebrities, media and the standard of living in majority minds, how we should live our life and how we should feel and what we should purchase in order to be happy and fit in society, but it isn't the way of ways, it's mostly all propaganda to sell you products and get you in debt at an early age, so you have to never stop working, to lock you in place so you don't have the real money and power later on in life when you grow up more and realize what is really going on.

Hurry up and settle down in your 20s and get in huge debt, before you actually realize that you lose all control by getting in debt and only the real money will give you real power. Also, people telling you constantly to work in quiet and let success do the talking, that's practically like saying, shut up and go to work. While in reality, speaking up and getting yourself, your products and your services and brands out there is the way to real riches and prosperity, not the so called American dream with a 30-year mortgage where the bank makes all the money, credit cards, 401k and student loan debt, those are all prison products, and are pushed on people at an early age taking advantage of our youth financially, which needs to stop, that is why I am bringing awareness to this topic in this book.

It is important to break out of the thinking that you need to be doing "The thing", and if you are not doing that, then you should be feeling guilty. It is probably something that came from the media or you've been brainwashed by your peers, who have been also brainwashed before the age of fourteen, that's when the human brain is most vulnerable to accept the facts and have them deeply sink into the subconscious mind for the rest of your life, that is why for generations things didn't really change much, until now, thank god for the connected age when we have more access to the truth and can research facts before we actually take them as it is. Make your own decisions. Be the captain of your own life and decisions.

You don't have to live where you live or stay in the job you have. Well, you might say: "but I have bills to pay", but understand that you've created the bills! You created liabilities that were probably pushed on you by media and other so called "trusted" information sources to believe it's necessary to have.

You don't have to work where you do or have a certain career - that is your mental picture pushing you to do so, you can move anywhere and have a life that you want now. You don't have to live where you live, it really is up to you to change it and you have the power to do that NOW.

Which parts of your life are draining you of the energy that can be used elsewhere? You don't have to sleep at certain times as creativity comes during odd hours. Sometimes you get creative bursts randomly, so start performing during those creative moments and capture them, optimize that time because that's when your brain is active to perform at its best.

Do it now! Don't wait for later. Later never happens and that's why people are stuck in a state where they are unhappy or unfulfilled with liabilities dragging them down. They make excuse after excuse as to why they are comfortable and get sensitive if you question them why.

Break out and seek freedom by changing your perspectives. For example, people say, "I don't have money to go where I always wanted to go, but this is a just an excuse. Look at how many people came from other countries, started with nothing and made a life they wanted for themselves. There is money abundance, particularly in America for those who really want it and are prepared to work for it. When you can understand that there are trillions of dollars in trade going around in the world every single day, you'll begin to see how anyone with an average intelligence in America or other first world country can achieve any kind of financial or other achievements if they just have the right mindset.

When looking at pictures of people doing something you would like to do or have, analyze your excuse and see where that limiting belief is really coming from because most of the time it is an easy fix. Our mind regularly runs in a user mode reacting automatically to the environment and conditions around us. Change your mindset and you will change your life. Instead switch it into super user mode so you can gain control of your mind and especially your attention and your time.

Attention is your most important asset so it is important to use it wisely. Like a budget or money, every time something is happening it is costing you your attention. When you watch a commercial or you're spending time on social media. The more attention you spend on things that don't get you to your goal, the more attention currency you have wasted.

Time is money and attention directed during that time is money. That is why attention directed into the right places will make money. It is also why multitasking isn't always as practical as we think it can be, because we think we are getting things done yet our attention is not directed towards any particular task at the time.

We constantly install time-wasting apps with attention grabbing alerts and watch cute videos of cats on YouTube, or even watching The Walking Dead on another screen. But which one of these tasks is ACTUALLY truly beneficial, besides self-indulgence on dopamine and other chemicals being released into our system?

Is this time being used to actually get tasks done that are productive in any way to get us to OUR goal that we have set up for ourselves? No, we are soaking up other peoples' agenda placed there to get them to THEIR goal to sell you THEIR content. Then people wonder why only two percent of the population is considered to be 'rich' financially. The reason for that is that the two percent know how to direct their attention towards the tasks that are beneficial for their agenda, not someone else's.

The rich get their own tasks done that benefit their goals, while using the masses by selling them content and product that they have created to utilize the massive scale formula. If you want to be successful then redirect your attention, which equals time, which equals money, towards productive tasks that will actually benefit you, like reading a book on an area of your interest or getting a project done. Once you force yourself with willpower to make this a habit, it becomes automatic. This is because our brains work as patterns and once a destructive or nonproductive habit is destroyed and replaced by a productive positive one, you will literally change your destiny.

THE BRAIN'S TWO SYSTEMS

The brain has a slow system that gives you control over things and a fast system that gets things done. For optimal success, it is important to integrate both systems into your daily life. Set a control system if it is a matter of other people giving you control on what you do and implement fast system to get things done.

If you are more of a slow system person then hire people with fast system in the brain to perform tasks while you oversee everything from a rational viewpoint. On the other hand, if you are a fast system person then get slow system people to keep you in control.

RUN DON'T WALK

Momentum is critical to your success. That's why you need to implement massive action towards the goal you are going after because if your energy is not dedicated to it, it will fail. Concentrate your energy on the goal you are after and don't get caught up in the meaningless things in life.

By trying to take care of everything or do everything at once your energy is split and nothing gets done. However, by focusing all of your energy on a particular task you could have achieved the one goal you are after.

PART

3

MINDSET FOR SUCCESS

NEUROSCIENCE IN BUSINESS

"We become, neurologically, what we think." – Nicholas Carr

Our brains feel comfortable, safe and happy when we do what others are doing. That's why we prefer brands that are popular. Established brands are often much more successful, as people, like sheep, flock to safety in numbers and the opinions of others. It's really our brain's survival mechanism because back in the day we were safe in numbers and couldn't get attacked by enemies or predators.

It takes a certain amount of time for our pragmatic brains to accept a product that solves certain problems. Marketing makes people think in a way that you desire for them to purchase the product from you. If it's unique and works on people's emotions, it's a great strategy. If you word your marketing correctly that can define a new category in people's minds and then you can dominate that category. Even if the product already existed, the way you present your new product can be in such a different way that people will be drawn to your product as it will create a new category in their mind. You can position it to be more intuitive, more fun or anything else that is desirable to a certain type of client or customer.

INSIDE AN ENTREPRENEUR'S MIND: RESILIENCE, FLEXIBILITY AND ADAPTABILITY

Before we dive into the mind of an Entrepreneur, let's firstly define what an Entrepreneur is:

- Choosing the marketplace

- Identifying the ideal customer

- Setting goals

- Building teams

- Understanding the competition

- Raising capital

- Embracing change

If people are doing good in your industry then there is a way for you to do well in it also. However too often we make excuses for ourselves that limit our ability to be successful. Carefully listen to what your excuses are and where they came from. Restructure your mindset to remove them if you want to succeed in your particular niche.

If some people are successful and you are not, then most likely they know something you don't know and all you have to do is find out what it is and apply it. Applying it into action is also a major key because if you know it but don't do it then nothing will happen. The mainstream education system was created decades ago however in a connected and advanced world, the answers lie in experience and self-learning, not just relying on answers in general education text books.

When you have an entrepreneurial mindset, you focus on outcomes instead of an output and you focus on contribution versus entitlement or a deserving attitude. You eliminate what is not needed and instead focus on what is needed to achieve the outcome you are after. You learn to make big decisions and take calculated risks even without an authority. From a personal perspective, you need to eliminate all other factors besides the goal you are after. You can make money working the harder, faster approach but if you want real financial security then you need to adopt an outcome-focused mind.

You might think bouncing to another industry is going to make you successful, but that is not necessarily true. You have to be successful from within and then you can succeed in almost any marketplace. There is a skill to the craft of what you are currently doing as well as a specific business or success skill. If you don't have the success skill you most likely are not going to be successful. Our school system teaches us how to be good at our craft but not the skills you need to be successful. You have to train yourself for that skills during a trial-error process of aiming ambitiously, failing and learning. That is how success skills are learned.

Once your mind is structured in this way, you will adopt the true essence of an Entrepreneur's mindset, meaning that you can be successful in many different types of businesses just by applying this universal mindset. It is the mindset of being the master of your own life in every aspect. As I always say, mastering every aspect of life and not just one aspect (i.e. financial or wealth) and neglecting other areas such as relationships or health, will not give you true success. True success lies in all areas of your life and any well-balanced Entrepreneur knows this. Imagine if your life is a wheel and part of that wheel is damaged - it will not spin. Refine every aspect of your life by learning from other people's successes and through your own trial and errors and you will live a happy and fulfilled life. Most people don't see that they have options besides what society tells them. Are you one of those people?

THE NOT SO SECRET TO THE GOOD LIFE.

"There is no elevator to success, you have to take the stairs" - *Ravina Shiyale*

Get off your chair or couch right now and go do what you know for a fact you should be doing. It's time to start following your intuition.

Why? Because it's a lot easier to have success than we are led to believe. We create our own reality so you just have to do what you think you should do, be persistent and believe in yourself.

And stop doing things that you know for a fact are destructive or are hindering you from achieving your goals. The choices that you make will shape your life. If you want a fulfilling life then do good (follow your intuition), implement the things that are right and do not implement the things that are not.

Growing up in an extreme in comparison to now

environment I've learned to understand that the external factors are not so much of an issue because you can overcome them with your willpower. The system that will work for you is to do what you feel is right: your intuition. For example, if you know that you have to spend quality time with your family then go do it, if you know you have to save money and not spend it, so do it. Or if you know that you need to get a better job or transition to more meaningful work, then go do it. If you know you have to learn a certain skill in order to get the job and do meaningful work you enjoy then go do it. Do it right now.

You are in charge of the decisions you make in your life, so why aren't you doing it? Nike's slogan 'Just Do It' has remained a world-renowned phenomenon because it's so simple yet so meaningful. It's not hard to just go and implement a certain action. What is really making it hard - is your own mind. Why are you battling your own self when you know for a fact what is good and right to do? Yes, our brains are wired to take an easy path in life sometimes but it's destructive and will not bring you prosperity and fulfillment. Implement the positive into action and it will become your life. That is how people who lead happy, fulfilled and meaningful lives do it. They are no different from you, they just simply implement positive actions into their life and that shapes their life with positive decisions to make it great. Nothing is in your way except your own self. Truly, look internally - all of the excuses that you are making are for the biggest reason because you don't want to do it and your brain wants to take an easy path. But you are in control of that. It is just a matter of priorities. Remove the things that are not right for you or your family.

Of course, it is ok to occasionally indulge and I believe that it can be productive to your success like spending quality time with your family, or exercising or pursing other interests. However, it is important to watch out when it becomes detrimental.

You might be thinking, well that's obvious! But the reality is, are you really implementing this simple strategy into your life in full? Are there areas where you can optimize this strategy better? Think about it.

THE BILLION-DOLLAR MINDSET

"If you are born poor it's not your mistake, but if you die poor – it's yours." -Bill Gates

It takes years to learn to play the piano but if you have learned for years, you can play it RIGHT NOW. It takes years of practice and learning to program, but a skilled developer can do it now because he already learned that skill through acquiring knowledge, training his mind and practicing to get it right.

Similarly, it takes years to master any skill but once you know it, you know it and you can perform it right now. High-level skills are in such high demand and are highly compensated for because of the years of work and experience that it took to get there. Some people choose not to take this route and simply end up paying others to perform the skill.

Your mind becomes what you are pursuing from repetition and perseverance. The same thing applies with a billion dollars. It takes time and mistakes and learning what works and what doesn't to get the strategies right but once you do, you can do it NOW with your mindset alone, and you can do it later, the second and the third time a LOT faster as you avoid the obstacles that you originally faced and conquered.

That is why your mind is your only true asset. All man-made materials were initially created by the mind. The mind creates all other assets, besides time (which is the second most valuable asset after the mindset). However, the right mindset using the time asset correctly can create any other material asset (including wealth) with ease. Like piano players, a trained mind will not hit the same bad keys over and over anymore. After they already went thought that process of training for years, the mind will hit the right keynotes and the music they are trying to create will be produced. The same goes for creating wealth and this is why the rich become richer and the poor become more poorer. It all comes down to the way we think and the way we train our mind.

FOUR STATES OF AWARENESS

When it comes to eliminating bad habits including focusing on non-value adding activities, and building positive new habits, it is important to understand the process of awareness. I myself am at the stage where I am constantly focused on implementing only positive action into my life.

Outlined below are the four steps.

- Consciously unaware - ignorant of the fact that we don't know how to do it or even have a problem

- Consciously aware- becoming aware that we don't know how to do it and taking the steps to fix it

- Subconsciously aware - practicing the skill or endeavor that we want to perform

- Subconsciously unaware - the skill becomes subconsciously and automatically performed

You can have hard time building neurological passages in your brain to make your skills habitual unless you learn to visualize. Our thoughts create the universe around us. Try thinking in a different way about the same thing and it will become it. Our fearful thoughts are just as powerful as our positive thoughts.

I believe that the reason older people want to settle down and get a nice comfy home and savings is to retreat. This is because the older you get the more obstacles you had to face throughout your life and you've used up all your energy to overcome them. We also have more fear with age as our brain is programmed to record every event that was negative and that has high levels of emotion attached to it. This phenomenon has evolved as a survival mechanism in the cave men era in order to survive during reoccurring negative events.

Negative thinking actually gives you insecurities so you can't think negatively and have a positive voice, make a positive impact on people and the world around you. The number one step is to go from consciously unaware of things (i.e. ignorant state) to a consciously aware state (i.e. when you become aware that the problem exists).

Then you start taking repeated actions to fix the problem. That is the subconsciously aware state where you train your subconscious mind to act differently, the way you want it to. Then you enter into the subconsciously unaware state which is when you perform actions you practiced automatically with your subconscious mind, like driving a car. This is how you become successful in life. I believe that if you focus on the negative things in your life that takes strength away from actually starting to have a positive impact on the world and having a voice.

THE POWER OF THE SUBCONSCIOUS MIND OVER THE CONSCIOUS.

Some studies show that subconscious mind is 30000 times more powerful than the conscious.

For decades, scientists have known that the subconscious mind is considerably more powerful than the conscious. Taking that in consideration, if you learn how to control your subconscious mind, you can actually possess the power of not just breaking bad habits by controlling your behavior but also fixing your belief system and getting rid of unwanted emotions.

In short, you can change almost anything if you learn how to master your subconscious mind but this cannot be done without understanding its rules. Indeed, there are a number of rules that govern the subconscious aspect of your brain and you need to be aware of what they are if you hope to control it.

Listed below are some important rules you should learn:

1. The first thing you should understand is the fact that your subconscious mind cannot differentiate between real situations and visualizations. For instance, when you watch a

102

horror movie you can feel your pulse racing even though you know you are not in any real danger. This is only because your subconscious cannot distinguish between imaginary and real situations.

This rule can come in handy as you can visualize what you want to be and your mind will automatically start working towards it.

2. An important rule that you need to be aware of is that the longer you let your subconscious mind believe something, the tougher it will get to alter this belief. It is the law of repetition. This gives your subconscious great power because it can force you to take actions based on those beliefs. Thus, learning how to control the subconscious mind gives you the ability to change your beliefs thereby impacting your decisions and actions in the future.

3. One of the most intriguing facts about the subconscious mind is that it will always prevail in conflicts with the conscious mind. If you are claustrophobic and you find yourself trapped in a small place, then you are going to get anxious and suffer from a panic attack even if you consciously try to convince yourself that there is nothing to be scared about. This is mostly because the subconscious mind is using its influence to weaken and control your conscious mind.

4. The greater effort your conscious mind makes; the lesser response you are going to get from your subconscious. For instance, you are trying hard to sleep consciously, but you are going to feel even more awake because you are making conscious effort. You will find it easier to sleep if you stop making conscious effort and don't think too much.

5. You can program the subconscious mind with the help of suggestions. This is the entire premise on which hypnosis is based as you send suggestions to your subconscious mind during this process. As long as the conscious mind is not supervising this process, your subconscious mind will accept all the suggestions you give it. This can make it easy for you to influence your behavior or change anything else you might want.

6. Time passes faster for your subconscious mind. Whenever you are doing something fun, time simply seems to fly by because you are not checking your watch after every few minutes. There is no sharp sense of time in the subconscious mind so it makes you feel like you have hardly spent any time doing the interesting activity. The same is applicable when you fall asleep. Your conscious mind is dormant when you are sleeping, but the subconscious is awake so you think you haven't slept much.

Understanding these rules governing the subconscious mind make it easier for you to know how it works and how you can control it for changing anything you want and apply it in your business and personal life to your advantage.

Knowledge is power and is in essence the building blocks for imagination and creativity. Knowledge storing and accumulation isn't about being smart. Being smart and intelligent is using your imagination and creativity. Knowledge is available everywhere for you to acquire and provides the building blocks for new inventions and accomplishments.

When problems arise, your brain starts sorting the information it has to find the best possible solution but the problem is that it only has the information you have giving it. Therefore, I can't stress enough on how reading books is the best thing you can do to improve yourself and your quality of life and those around you.

EMOTIONAL INTELLIGENCE

"When dealing with people, remember you are not dealing with creatures of logic, but with creatures of emotion." -Dale Carnegie

Eighty percent of success lies in an interesting concept called emotional intelligence. Only about twenty percent or so of success is directly attributed to your IQ level. But emotional intelligence is not taught in the traditional schooling system and is something we need to seek out for ourselves.

When it comes to marketing, brands need you to stay emotional in order to sell products as it is the emotional part of the brain that is triggered to make purchases.

By consuming content on TV, your reptilian part of the brain is activated over and over and is trained to purchase or make impulsive decisions. That's why commercials are shown during football games and movies when you are feeling most emotional so your reptilian brain can register the product emotionally, usually with repetition over and over so that it sinks deep into our subconscious mind.

When you see it you automatically trust that product or

person and you purchase from them or from that brand. One of the most deeply held secrets to achieving great wealth is to repeatedly show yourself or your product while people are in a highly emotional state such as watching a game of sports or relaxing having a beer. With time and repetition, the reptilian brain registers that person or product as a trusted source and starts to really connect with them or the product.

On a chemical level, we get addicted and feel the need to purchase, that's why people scream when they see a celebrity. Why wouldn't you do that to a regular person? Don't get caught up in praising 'celebrities' or so called experts who get people in an emotional state to sell them themselves and their products while prospering dramatically financially. Yes, they know they are doing this and they purposely use it against the masses. It's not by accident. This is how ultra-wealth is made.

Do I do this? To a degree, I have implemented it with my business. You have to understand emotions, psychology and human behavior in order to truly succeed in business. That is what I am teaching here and I want everyone to have access to this knowledge because knowledge is power. I want everyone to realize how to use it to make their business better and more prosperous.

Everyone who is reading this book will know this secret and

should use it to their advantage and tell others. By helping others, we will help the human kind and the world around us. Energy exerted from you eventually has to come back, so what you give will come back in equal amount. The more you help, the more abundant you will be in your own life.

THE BATTLE OF THE MINDSETS

"Our greatest battles are those with our own minds." – Jameson Frank

Life used to be a battle of biological states of different and same species. But now it's becoming a battle of the mindsets, opinions or the way people think. We are essentially testing on each other to see which mindset is more suitable to persevere and evolve, this is how evolution of the mind is created and what I believe is the meaning of life. We are battling with opinions and different views on life such as political ideas, sport teams, product and service choices and personal opinions.

How you perceive life in your mind is based on your accumulated beliefs and values from sources you have been exposed to. For instance, when you hang out with other people around you they all have different views on life and the concept of 'reality' means something different to each one of them.

Have you noticed how so many things in this world are a fight or competition be it computer games, sports, politics, countries and people, racing, playing chess, etc.? We can't physically hurt each other anymore legally but now it's becoming more of a battle of mindsets. In the corporate world or in sales and marketing, competition is huge in just about any niche you look at in the marketplace.

So why are we brainwashed by nature to do this? It's to test each other to evolve the more suitable mindset. We are used as vessels to participate in this, while exposed to different environments, conditions and data. We think that life should be the way we think it is and we are so convinced that sometimes people are even ready to harm another person if they don't share the same view of the world. Again, turn on the news. It's really on a barbaric level. In the future, I believe that we will evolve to start testing consciously and not subconsciously. Testing will evolve to being performed on machines and on the cloud.

Don't be a test vessel lab rat, you can always just relax and be happy without competing so hard or trying to prove something so hard as it's just in your mind. It's really deeply

109

just insecurities that drive us so hard to money and power. If you are actually aware of this - you can be happy, relaxed, feel secure and appreciative in the moment. I am not saying don't strive to be a better person, just know what is going on in your body and mind and why you are doing it.

WANT DIFFERENT RESULTS? THEN LEARN TO SHIFT YOUR MINDSET

"Once your mindset changes, everything on the outside will change along with it" – Steve Maraboli

It is important to create the right psychology and eliminate seeking immediate wins or financial gains and instead become a producer of product and service for as large of clientele as possible. The more people that you serve and bring value to, or whose life you make easier, the more asset value you will build for your business. Make that psychological shift to set yourself apart from everyone else and create loyal fans as customers, just like companies such as Apple have.

One of the keys to being a successful entrepreneur for me is not settling based on one opinion or roadblock. If somebody says to me "no" I look at where they are in their own business or life and if they have been saying no to themselves all these years, they will sometimes just be self-projecting onto you. Just because their psychology has been dragging them down, don't automatically apply it to yourself by accepting what they have told you. A real entrepreneur has their own opinion about what can be done so go to multiple sources and combine the information you have gathered to calculate the best way of action and then execute it.

If something is not working out on one level go to the core of the problem and eliminate it at the core. For instance, if you do not get approved at the bank you can evaluate your credit by going to a non-profit credit counselor. Take action to clean your credit from the core and then come back and you will be approved. And don't say to yourself it's easier said than done because it's not – if you actually do it you will be surprised how it can turn out. When you do things people tend to help and the system starts working for you instead of against you. When you do nothing about it, it can become a vicious circle of never ending problems that most likely you alone created to begin with. Remember to look in the mirror for the real cause of these problems.

If you have a roadblock it's often because of something else that is stopping you and not necessarily the problem you are facing. That's why it is important to evaluate what is truly in the way of getting this done or what is truly required to accomplish this task. If your marketing efforts are not producing results, is it likely because you cheaped out on marketing experts or your strategy is not suitable for your business.

For example, are you throwing a lot of money and time on marketing that doesn't work for your business? If so, re-evaluate from the core and then adjust your strategy accordingly to fit your business niche and solve that problem. Remember, the world doesn't care about your ideas and goals, it cares about how much value you can provide. If there is something you think you can't control usually look around to find other reasons why. Don't just bluntly look at the specific scenario over and over.

Why do some businesses and products succeed while others fail? Because some are simply better, some products work better than others or the level of service provided is better or offered at a more competitive price than the others. They provide more value to people and businesses. Always aim to deliver value.

But sometimes strategies are similar and nobody knows why one became more popular than the other and this usually

112

comes down to social interactions. Word of mouth marketing is more targeted than any other method. Harnessing the power of why people talk about certain things or not, is the key. To truly understand what causes people to share their opinions, views and recommendations you have to look at both their failures and successes and see what characteristics lead to success in most cases. My belief is that virality isn't born it's made. If someone figures out how to make something to be talked about they will succeed.

NEGATIVE ENERGY IS INFECTIOUS

"Positive vibes", is one of my favorite things to say now when I speak to my family, girlfriend, friends or anyone else to quickly switch them into a warm, fuzzy feeling mode, but it's of course not always the solution, because sometimes you have to listen to people and give valuable feedback if they are trying to vent to you about something.

We are wired to think negatively more so than positively naturally because back in the caveman era we needed to remember negative experiences so that we would learn from them and not do them again in order to survive. I keep repeating myself in the book with some statements such as these, simply because repetition sinks in our subconscious and becomes automatic and it's the best way to learn.

But now in the modern age of course it is sometimes useful to be negative still but for the most part it's a destructive way of thinking because our environment has changed so much. So don't act negatively in times of negative change. Instead collect your thoughts and act positively in the way that will shape that situation to give it the best outcome possible. In business, this becomes a challenge during the hard times. It's best not to react automatically to the negative situation instead act with a conscious mind.

BENEFITS OF KEEPING A POSITIVE MINDSET

Do you see your glass as being half full or half empty? Is it your habit to concentrate more on the problems than on the blessings? Your positive or negative thinking is not just a personality trait; it can actually have an impact on your physical and mental health and also the direction of your life. There are a lot of people who consider it a mistake to be optimistic because they believe it to be a way to hide from the reality, ignorance can be bliss but it doesn't produce results. However, the truth is that a positive outlook can go a long way in keeping you healthy and can provide a lot of benefits.

So, if you are wondering why you should stay positive, here are some excellent reasons that can convince you:

- Keeps your heart healthy

Positive thinking is not just good for your mind; it is also beneficial for your heart. When you are optimistic your heart health gets a boost and you are at a reduced risk of cardiovascular disease. So why not look at things through rose-colored glasses ones in a while or more so often?

- Beneficial for your relationships

If you are a positive thinker, you are going to have better luck in love and relationships. There are a number of reasons behind this phenomenon. When you are a positive person you are more satisfied in your relationship as opposed to pessimists because you tend to focus on the good aspects rather than the bad. Furthermore, you will also become more accepting of flaws and won't look at them in a negative way.

- Reduces stress levels

Positive thinking has been associated with lower stress levels because optimistic people are less likely to suffer from depression and anxiety. Worry and negative thoughts usually cause stress but positive people find it easier to overcome it. Good thoughts are going to drive your stress away and make you a better person.

- Creates a better first impression

You will leave a better first impression on people when you make positive thinking your priority. It is natural for people to be attracted to friendly and kind personalities and that's exactly what you will be. This first impression can pave the way for better relationships in the future.

- You become more resilient

Your ability to cope with problems improves when you look at things positively. You can face a trauma or crisis with resolve and strength when you see the good side of everything. With positive thinking, you will ensure that you don't fall apart in the face of stress and can carry on to overcome any adversity. Every time you encounter a challenge, your positive thinking will drive you to look for a way to fix the problem rather than give up hope.

- Motivation and success

It is a fact that positive thinking people are more likely to be successful as compared to pessimists. This is due to the fact that a positive attitude will automatically give you motivation to achieve your goals. You will believe that success becomes easier and it is not as difficult as you have been led to believe.

- Attracts positive events

Many of you would be familiar with the 'law of attraction'? With positive thoughts, feels and vibrations you can create your own reality, just as you want it to be. The main principle that governs this law is that like attracts like. This means that if you think positive, positive things are going to happen to you. If you make this kind of thinking a habit, good things will be attracted to your life automatically.

Hence, staying positive keeps you healthy and alive and strengthens your mental resolve. It also paves the way for a better future so it is better to be an optimist rather than a pessimist.

THE POWER OF VISUALIZATION REALLY DOES WORK

"Visualize this thing that you want, see it, feel it, believe in it. Make your mental blue print, and begin to build." -Robert Collier

Visualizing things that you really want to happen in your future does really work and here is why. Everything that is man-made once came from an idea be it cities, books, music, cars or fashion. Visualizing and materializing what's not there yet is creativity and you can visualize things that aren't there yet and then implement them into action. The brain already has an ability to bring the future into the present. That is a natural instinct to predict danger and is a genetic gift that is a result of many years of evolution. So use that to your advantage to create things in your life. Visualize the improved feature and create it by focusing on what it can be, what it might be and how it can be. And then, of course, practice it. Practice visualizing things in the future the way you want them to be.

When you receive impulses and ideas strike - take advantage of them right away. Don't wait because the chances of you remembering them or recreating them later are slim. Seize the moment and record it or write it down, better yet tell or explain it to someone else. Make sure your devices are around like a phone, voice recorder, computer or pen and are ready to capture the idea fast, because a few minutes of looking for a pen or booting up the computer can cost you the idea.

I personally carry a voice recorder everywhere and bust it out the second an idea strikes. You know what they always say: "visualize yourself already in possession of the things you want." Well the miracle of creativity is when you start with nothing and create something. It does work, simply because evolution gave our brain a gift, or evolved it to a point where it can see the future. Over the years it has evolved into imagination and creativity so this can be used in the sense that we can visualize the things we want and our brain attains it. After all, our minds are currently the most powerful instrument in the universe so use it to create the reality that you want.

ACHIEVING PEACE OF MIND WITHOUT JUDGMENT

How do I obtain peace? Why can't I ever seem to find peace? These are some of the common things that people ask on a regular basis. Inner peace and the means of achieving it are deemed to be the most sought after secrets in the area of mental health.

It is with good reason that we ask these questions because we all need some moments of peace if we don't want to slip into depression or anxiety. The problem is that it is easier said than done. There is nothing that can be purchased to gain inner peace.

It is ironic that we become even more frustrated in the pursuit of peace. This is especially true in moments when you are truly tired, hurt, distressed or exhausted. When you genuinely feel bad, you want to have some peace. The definition of peace is different for everyone. Some view it as a nice conversation with your partner, an uninterrupted day at the office or even a walk at the beach. However, there are still times when you are walking on the beach and your mind is uneasy or you are speaking to your spouse, but you don't feel comfortable. So why does this happen? Well this mostly happens because the definitions of peace listed above are merely peaceful situations. They don't necessarily bring you peace. In order to achieve real peace of mind, you have to have a peaceful mindset first. A mindset that is unconditional or not based on any external conditions to feel peace. These situations you have imagined make it easier for you to relax and feel at ease but they still don't bring peace. In simple terms, they are just the outer weather of your personality and it is the internal weather you have to focus on for the purpose of achieving true peace of mind. The definition I like most is "peace is a moment without judgment." What does this mean to you? Most people would just scoff and consider them a bunch of fancy words that don't really mean much. But this is not the case. You need to think objectively in order to truly understand the meaning behind these words. What sounds more peaceful to you? Feeling compassionate and gentle towards yourself when you are down or fighting against it and cursing yourself for whatever caused the feelings in the first place?

It is easy to get even more frustrated when you are wishing the negative feelings away only to realize that this is easier said than done. It is natural for us to berate any feelings of anxiousness or sadness that we encounter in everyday life, but we do not realize that by doing that, it only prevents you from understanding your feelings and connecting with yourself. Just because you close your eyes doesn't mean the problem will go away. Darkness doesn't make objects disappear. Thus, you have to find a better way to deal with it and find the inner peace you seek.

Rather than evaluating your feelings and passing any judgment, it is a better idea to accept them as they are. When you accept, what is happening inside of you, it will automatically put a stop to the inner war. Instead of fighting, you should connect with your feelings and this will provide you with the peace you have wanted because you finally achieve true understanding. You become closer to yourself, which allows you to understand who you are and how to heal yourself. In essence, you have to learn to let the negativity go and let the positivity in to achieve a peace of mind.

There has never been a novel about good marriage because it might seem boring and is like the perfect life nobody wants to hear about. People want to hear about drama, violence and other barbaric actions. I believe that our brains have been really conditioned by the media to stay in the state where we are emotional because that drives sales. However, in the near future that will change especially if people start exercising their frontal lobe more with books and other positive materials and that way they will be able to control their emotions and create real piece from the inside.

YOUR MIND VIBRATES WITH OTHER PEOPLE

"Everything is energy and that's all there is to it." -Albert Einstein

When you are in the crowd, your mind becomes as weak as the weakest person in that crowd. That's why public speakers, politicians, motivational speakers, all use this technique to brainwash masses easily in those situations. You are more likely to go with the flow and do what everyone else is doing in the crowd than stand up and challenge what's being said. Top speakers and artists in the world are some of the biggest income earners. Their shows are a massive sales movement to your emotional part of the brain and nothing is more emotional than music.

Our brains vibrate with other people we interact with so it's important to think about where your beliefs are really coming from. Is it something that a friend has told you? That's often the case and is why being around people that are not aligned with your goals in life is hindering your ability to move you towards those goals. There are people who will try to make you think in the way that will not get you to where you are going. Have you ever thought something and been so convinced of it but unsure as to where that thought came from?

Well you need to ask yourself who exactly told you that this was correct, or this is the way to think or live. Was it a jealous friend or a guy on TV who is interested in making money from you? The answer is most likely all of the above. And there are so many more people everywhere around you who are trying to get the money out of you by psychologically trying to convince you what they are offering is worth more than your cash, or brings more value into your life. But is it?

If you think about it, on a psychological level, things that are of extreme value in our man-made reality are actually insignificant in the ultimate reality. Think of gold and diamonds for instance, prestigious brands that you pay several times more for than a regular product, prestigious neighborhoods or some other things of so called value. Are they really more valuable or was it just established that way in the brain of human beings.

I use TO a TREE concept to test and crack things of this nature. For instance, would it matter to a tree or not. Does gold matter to a tree? In this case no it doesn't. That means it's a psychologically established value by humans that in ultimate reality doesn't mean the same. Does water matter to a tree – yes, to survive. So water is a real physical value that helps you in reality. Does a Gucci or a Prada purse matter to a tree, no it doesn't, so it's not of a real value, it's a psychological brand-washed value.

REALITY DISTORTION FIELD

The only limits are the ones you make in your mind.

Reality distortion field is when you refuse to accept any limitations standing in the way of your goals and ideas. That is what creates disruptive innovation that really propels evolution forward. I believe that modern evolution is happening in large as a matter of our free will and constant mindset improvement. Also for me when I am working on managing a project it's like a force of nature that helps get to the end result despite the odds against it happening. That is why investors often look at an important factor of ignorance on a positive way in a team or a team leader, as it acts as a refusal of the so called current reality standing in the way of their ideas being implemented.

Real leadership is the ability to convince yourself that any difficulty is not a limitation and to have the ability to convince others about it as well. That is how leaders get people to accomplish what they have envisioned. And it's usually the most challenging part to set the mind of other people to your reality distortion frequency. If this is accomplished, a bullet-proof team is born capable to overturn projects of tremendous magnitudes.

SWITCHING FROM A LOOSER TO A WINNER STATE IN LIFE

"Winners see the gain, losers see the pain." -Shiv Khera

We put ourselves into either a looser or winner state in life by the constant actions that we choose out of our thoughts and the repetition of those actions.

If we are in the looser state we are unhealthy with bad eating habits, sleeping cycle, bad friends, unsatisfying work, bad relationships, broken finances, and broken spirituality. I call this state the sick mind state. This is a vicious cycle and usually comes from inner insecurities. For instance, if you have a financial insecurity, you think you are poor and the work you do isn't what you want to do and it doesn't produce

126

much income. So you focus on these thoughts and tell yourself that you are that person.

I am poor, I am a looser and my work sucks. Well this mindset also creates bad eating habits, drinking habits and attracts people with the same mindset because misery likes company. Your spirituality is broken and so is your physical body from damaging it with your unhealthy thinking. And because your mind now is in a bad environment it keeps staying in that state of sickness.

However, if you dig deeply into your mind and are honest with yourself about what is really causing it for you, what is the insecurity that you need to eliminate in order to break out of this state? For instance, if you have insecurity of under accomplishing financially, you feel like you have to overcompensate and buy a big house to be successful in order to be happy. Then you realize that you are not accomplishing it right now so you make yourself sick and take away strength and happiness from the now and that puts you into this vicious cycle that I have just described.

So how do I break out of this? Well, you target that particular insecurity and tell yourself that you don't need to think that way because it is causing you damage at the present moment. Then you eliminate it like a weed. After that you no longer need to turn to unhealthy eating or drinking patterns to cover up your insecurity, so your body in turn gets into better shape and that provides your mind with a better, healthier environment so you start thinking even healthier.

After that success breeds success. It compounds; as your body becomes stronger your mind gets rid of some more bad thinking that was leading you to problems in relationships or friends that are bad influencers. When you fix that part of your life, your brain sky rockets to a healthier way of thinking, then you gain spirituality and your finances are improving through a healthier mindset. Now you're at the stage where you can buy that house you wanted earlier but it's not that important to you anymore because your brain has more meaningful goals in your life now. Then you start doing meaningful work that brings joy and fulfillment into your life and your brain is a lot healthier again and that creates a spinning wheel of life with every aspect of your life being healthy. It gains momentum very quickly and everything starts manifesting and improving, immediately. This is a quick guide for switching from a looser to a winner state in life.

HOW TO BECOME A MILLIONAIRE: THE

ULTIMATE WEALTH FORMULA

"Don't let fear of losing be greater than excitement of winning." -Robert
Kiyosaki

Don't merely trade time for money. Don't spend another day making a few bucks with no leverage or growth opportunity. Instead invest the time into yourself and your business for exponential growth opportunities. Invest as much as possible of your time and money into opportunities and assets that can generate income.

It's not really an investment if it doesn't make you money, so invest into projects, business, your personal skills and development, books, mentors and networks of people you work with and surround yourself with. These are exponential appreciation compound assets that pay off dramatically. Instead of wasting all of your energy and time on trying to produce an hourly income to make ends meet, invest your time into growth opportunities. For example, instead of making a down payment on a house, take that money and purchase a project that can generate income.

Don't retrieve constantly and waste your valuable time and energy on contracting and constantly running away and saving, instead invest everything into growth and expansion. Expand, don't contract if you want to get rich, you can't get rich running away. See that's where most people have the wrong mentality, a penny saved is a penny. First make a million then save a million, don't save pennies, don't make large personal purchases until you've made it, otherwise you never will. Don't keep purchasing status items to display, instead purchase assets that will generate income and don't just invest into something that will preserve money, invest into things that will generate money. Saving money is not growth it's also retreating. Yes, it's nice to save after you have achieved your financial goals but everyone is trying to save before they have achieved them and the reality is that there is nothing to save.

So take all you have now in terms of time, energy and money and invest into yourself, your networks, skills, projects, startups or whatever your endeavor is and keep at it. After you are generating large amounts of incomes keep reinvesting a large percentage back into the game to grow your income, while spending much less percentage on your lifestyle.

PEOPLE ARE POOR BECAUSE THEY

WANT TO BE RICH

"People label themselves poor therefore they are." – Vitaly Samonov

If you strive to be rich that automatically makes you not rich at the present moment mentally you don't think of yourself as a rich person and not just financially of cause but this can be in every aspect of life. If you keep trying to get rich all the time you will never become, as at any level you personally decide if you are rich and fulfilled or not.

Also, constantly trying to get rich is a selfish and self-indulging goal, instead trying to provide value on large scale with your service, content or product should be your goal and then you will get vastly rewarded financially and otherwise by the law of compensation. Building others up with doing things you love and helping other people solve their problems will build wealth in this world and for yourself and your family. Mentally and materially that will bring riches all around. If your goal is to buy a nice car, that will not bring fulfillment ultimately as you are not putting the dedication and love to what you are doing to get the car rather you are putting the efforts and mental concentration into getting the possession itself, which actually will make you less rich as it's a bad investment. Almost any assets you acquire built by

131

others will make you do less good financially as mostly it's a liability that will rid you of money instead of being an investment. Maintenance that comes with many possessions in the long run rids you of money and yes this does include real estate and buying a house. If you are buying a house for personal use it's not a great investment like most pushed to think by the banks who want to make money on you selling it as an American Dream, actually a 30 year mortgage is the worst financial decision of a lifetime, the way to actually make money with real estate would be investing in multicomplex apartments and renting them out, which also is a very complicated process and has to be a deal because again you can lose a lot of money on maintenance and many other expenses. So for me, providing value and concentrating on giving, yes here comes the often heard motivational statement "Give and you shall receive", truly genuinely shift your mind to give value to others without thinking of self-indulging goals and see the positive results pour into your life. This has been my secret for success and I highly recommend adopting this kind of mentality.

GROWTH MINDSET VS. FIXED MINDSET

Real growth usually comes during the process where it feels like you are taking three steps forward and two steps back. Every start-up or business goes through its foggy or difficult periods. People will persevere only if they perceive failure as learning.

What seem to be people's problems can actually be environmental problems. If you are wanting to break through these tough roadblocks, then design and rearrange the environment that makes bad behaviors undesirable or impossible. Change - isn't an event, it's a process and once you start, it starts feeding on itself. The successful tomorrow is successful today. If you are not going to be taking action to be successful today you will not be tomorrow.

Keep pushing through the roadblocks and look at the growth opportunities in order to take your business to the next level.

PART 4

BUSINESS SUCCESS

THE REAL FORMULA I USE FOR SUCCESS IN BUSINESS

Motivation can only get you so far. Once it inspires you to act, you need to act correctly and to know how to act correctly will save you years of headache that others went though, including myself, to make things work.

So, I am going to reveal a business model, or the formula in other words, that I utilize in my business to be successful. Wishing and trying to get rich doesn't work as it's a selfish act, and one is a fool to think they have made it by displaying expensive badges for others to see. You can only truly get rich by providing real value to others.

Here's how to get started:

• Define your market niche, which is precisely what you are going to do in detail. The more precise and detailed your niche is, the better chance you have of success because you will not want to be competing with Goliath who dominates the whole market place. Then accurately define your audience. What type of person will be using your product or service? Describe them, envision that person. What do they do? Where do they hang out? How do they dress? What do they like and dislike? What is their average income? The more statistics you have of your exact target customer, the better you can envision your product.

• Define what your target market needs - what is missing in that market niche? What are their needs and how can you solve them? How can you improve the current product on the market to make your clients' life easier, even if you can take an existing product and improve it by ten percent and make it better for your specific niche of people, that's fantastic! You don't always need to reinvent the wheel.

• Define your value proposition. What value are you providing? Is it even valuable at all? Again don't think about your dreams, it's about adding value to people and making their lives easier.

• Specify your Minimum Viable Product (MVP). What are you going to build with minimum features that people need and will want to use? It needs to be something that will benefit them better or in a different way than already existing products and services in the same market.

• Create your MVP prototype with great user interface design. Make it incredible, special and epic! Go all the way, thinking not about what you want but what that client that you envisioned earlier in your mind will actually want.

• Test the validity of your product or service. That was just a so-called preparation phase, the moment of truth is to see in reality and test if your envisioned client really wants or needs what you have to offer. Is it going to benefit him or her at all? After you get to test your MVP with customers, carefully collect feedback by asking or testing the statistics. I prefer real interactions with clients and getting their feedback, that way they stay loyal and see that we, as a company, actually care about providing them with real value that they need. And rapidly evolve your product. Customers will not only stay and use your product or service but engage in a viral factor that will automatically grow your product or service.

And that is why you need a bulletproof team. It's not your team size but rather their agility that is the key factor, because speed is important in a David vs. Goliath battle. That is how disruptive technologies are created, real value is provided into the marketplace and of course you get vastly compensated during the process.

DISRUPTIVE INNOVATION

"I have not failed. I've just found 10,000 ways that won't work." -
Thomas A. Edison

Disruptive marketers are bringing the industrial age to an end. Don't be set with both feet firmly in the 20th Century, as the creative and connected age has begun. Design is at the center of all human experience. Agile development is constantly improving and that's the key to innovate and come up with new strategies. Saying "this is how we always did it" is the enemy of success in the creative age. Soon disruptive innovators will completely recreate the way we were used to thinking in the industrial age of large corporations. Empathy, design and emotional intelligence are key factors to disruptive marketing and technology and lead to the development of almost anything we can imagine. You just have to believe that all possibilities are available to you. Marketing was drastically different in the 1950's when there were three channels on TV and it was dominated by those few who had access to that kind of power. Now a lot of companies still use the same approach but things have surely changed, people don't want ads, they don't want to be distracted from their daily lives. How many times do you really click on ads online or

140

elsewhere? We learn to tune them out and really we mostly distrust the ads. There is so much noise out there today and brands competing to be seen that when everyone is shouting the only way to get attention is to whisper.

Imagination is the key factor to disruptive technology. Imagine what doesn't exist in the world of real value right now and then make it happen. That is the true innovation. It doesn't have to be a complete new technology, product or industry. It can be an improvement. You can imagine an improvement that people really need and want and make it happen.

A smart creative individual combines marketing, design, and development expertise. The reason companies grew so large in the past is because they used to have one type of person for one profession and now whole departments can be done by a few people or even only one, with current analytics, technology feedback and other software available.

THE SECRET OF BRANDS AND CELEBRITIES

"You're only given a little spark of madness. You mustn't lose it." -
Robin Williams

Some people will disagree with me for giving out some of
these secrets I have discovered, as they say don't give out all
of your strategies. However, I think we live in a world now
where we have to work together not in secret or silos and not
against each other. Dictatorship is of the past and
cooperation is the future.

So here is what I have discovered as a really big money
strategy that the wealthy use:

The steps to monetize the masses are: you get people to
become aware of you and your product and then you get
them to know you by constantly exposing your brand or
product. People develop love in their brain on a chemical
level for celebrities or popular brands if they are constantly
getting exposed to it. It can build credibility and they will start
to like you and trust you. The trust is built through repetition,
the brand or celebrity starts monetizing and selling you their
product or service. That's where you are chemically

conditioned into purchasing through feelings like love and trust. And Hollywood, glorifies feelings as something super special and been pushing on us feelings packed propaganda sense we were little children to keep up locked in the emotion product purchasing state.

Why do you love a certain brand or a celebrity? Why do you trust them and watch their movies or listen to their music? Is it because you will appear cooler or more elite by your association with them? Perhaps it fits your personality, lifestyle or personal style. Either way, because we have been exposed to it enough it has created neuro passages in our brain that release chemicals whenever we hear or associate ourselves with that certain celebrity or a brand.

People obsess over certain celebrities or brands but really what is it that makes them so great? I suggest loving your family and yourself and what you are doing, don't get to obsessed with brands and celebrities (who are really just normal people in the spotlight) as it's only a marketing trick. And this has been a strategy for many years but it's changing now. I believe that brands in the future will not use this strategy but rather a more legitimate strategy like actually providing you with real value instead of imagined and psychological value. This will help make this world a better place because it will actually have more value in it.

ACTION TRUMPS KNOWLEDGE

It's not a matter of how smart you are or how much knowledge you can accumulate but rather the actions that you are implementing into your life and how quickly you can achieve the intended outcome. For instance, an athlete doesn't need to have a really high IQ but because so much work is performed into their life physically and mentally to make the body in such a shape, they are really highly compensated.

Compare this to an employee who is very low paid with no skills needed prior to starting the job. No neurological passages have been wired for many hours of practice nor have they needed to invest into self-development as an expert so that's why they get paid a very small amount. Also they can read one hundred books and be very knowledgeable but if they are not implementing it into a real action in their life, they are not getting paid for their knowledge or expertise. If they are not providing value to others with their knowledge they are not going to monetize properly on it. So choose a job or niche for your business that you are good at, think what you have practiced in your life most and implement that business into a real action to provide that expertise to others and you will be highly compensated.

ONE THOUSAND IDEAS

"Ideas are the currency of the 21st century." - Claudia Azula Altucher

Don't work on only one idea and think you will be a billionaire. Innovate and try different things. For me, I have looked back and just in the past few years we have done over 170 projects. Starting from the smallest things to multi-million dollar projects for other people and for myself and my team. Don't get stuck on one thing as your first ideas are not always that great because you have not yet exercised your idea muscle and haven't executed many ideas yet into reality to test them out to see what actually works.

If you don't test your ideas through, it's hard to see what is really needed or wanted in the marketplace or what is suitable for current demand or technology etc. I would just keep having thousands of ideas and hire people to have ideas and write them down. Have ideas, have idea reproduction with each other and produce new ideas, combine ideas, combine ideas from different industries, make them all work together and test them out in reality. Yes, it will take time and money but that is why you need to hire people to test your ideas. Hire teams just for a couple of ideas that you have combined.

Don't be afraid to try. If you fail you will only grow. Just keep evolving and learning and applying your knowledge from that test run of projects to your next project. Knowledge and experience of experimenting with ideas and projects will get you eventually to the one that can potentially pick up good traction and then put all of your money and efforts into it, hire more people and involve investors to put their time and budget into it because people will see the potential with traction already being there. If you've crossed the gap between struggle and traction, people will want to be a part of it, and then eventually you can join the unicorn club.

HIERARCHY STRUCTURE IS NOT THE FUTURE

"The greatest king of the kingdom is the one who serves." -Matthew 23:11

If the authority says so then it must be true, right? Well that's a lazy mindless way out of thinking for yourself. Hierarchies in society date all the way back to tribal ages when the leader of a tribe was selected on being physically and mentally suitable to protect the tribe in case of danger.

But to a certain degree, this type of hierarchy still exists. For instance, people of authority such as doctors are not questioned by their decisions and therefore potential errors are getting through. The same goes for people on TV with a perceived authority to sell products – people trust their opinion as being credible and correct so they go ahead and buy their product. They use celebrities in commercials to endorse products but really, they are not the experts in what they are selling.

There are a lot of self-made perceived authoritative figures out there and they build authority by doing self-PR and marketing of themselves to sell you a product or service. Do your own research before you fall for these kinds of people. In the future I believe that a more cooperative approach will become the way to work like communities that carefully decide and work as a team without just praising one person or seeing the one key person as an authority. We are already seeing this at the workplace. For example, Toyota employees are encouraged to say what improvements they would suggest for their products. In the future we will rely more on the voice of the people in the community with a common goal rather than an authorized leader of that community.

LEADERSHIP

When you are a leader your confidence in your endeavor is so strong that others are convinced that that is the way and they follow your direction. That is why you shouldn't question your vision and don't try to get validation from others to persevere.

Be true to your vision. Boldness has power. When you boldly push forward with a lot of action and momentum, others simply start to believe that path as well. If you start questioning yourself, then others will question your idea, path or vision.

BURY YOUR COMPETITION AND HATERS WITH ACTION

Advertise yourself, your product and your service. Don't be shy to over advertise and don't stand back, do not conform to others' thinking or think that others will think less of you and don't seek approval from others to take action. Always over promise and then you will have an obligation to over deliver. Think outrageously, post on social networks as much as possible, advertise yourself, your products and your services aggressively. The more you do, the more action you put into it, the better chance there is for a result. Here is a formula I use: fail, fail, fail, succeed, fail, fail, fail, succeed. So if you do three actions and fail every time the ultimate result is fail, but if you do four actions then you will succeed. If you do eight actions you will succeed twice. Just do more and don't be afraid, the only thing stopping you really is yourself and once you understand this, you can do anything. Everyone is trying to avoid negative experience but if you do that, then chances of your success are very slim. You must fail and in fact Warren Buffet doesn't even invest in people who haven't failed at least twice.

Your comfort zone will not give you any results so don't keep contracting back into it. You need to keep expanding. Expand and then save, don't keep contracting and saving with no action and low or no income and no output because nothing will happen. Bury your competition and your haters with ACTION. Do they hate you? If so, do more. They will eventually give up and follow you and your advice. Do your clients want and expect a great product? Then over promise and over deliver, don't be afraid to promise incredible results that will set the bar for you and your team. Brag a little. Forget balance, concentrate and produce massive action and you will start seeing massive results. If you want a mediocre life, implement mediocre action, it is as simple as that. There is nothing wrong with a comfortable relaxing life if that is your goal, but if you want massive success you must take massive action. If your goals and dreams are high, expect massive production from yourself and your team. They will call you crazy first but later they will call you a genius.

TRUSTWORTHINESS IN BUSINESS AND LIFE

"Trust takes years to build, seconds to break, and forever to repair" –
Amy Rees Anderson

I can't emphasis enough the importance that trustworthiness plays in both business and personal life. To express true genuine trust is to win a partner, people or business contacts and develop long-term relationships and repeat clients.

Integrity is the biggest ingredient that runs a successful business and relationships. Because like the laws of nature the more you give, the more you will receive back. That's how healthy business and romantic relationships work. I have been in a successful relationship for a long time and in business for even longer and I can tell you now that this is full and unquestionable truth.

There are people who think they are entitled to take from others close to them or from business partners and clients, but they always lose in the end. I believe that the most important aspect of having a good life, healthy relationships and a thriving business is to be trustworthy and give, and not always seek to take.

Don't expect to take every opportunity that presents itself as you are robbing yourself of connections and relationships in the future that could be strong and beneficial. From personal experience I highly encourage others to give. You will have to pay for it some other way and usually more, because those things are compounded by nature, good deeds are compounded and so are the bad ones, and that's why by damaging your relationships and business relationships you could very well end up alone and broke. Do things for people, send a recommendation or help out when they need something. Then you will be building for yourself a network of people who care and give back. Your network is your net worth so invest into your network of people by providing help, building trust and showing integrity.

DON'T BARK BACK AT YOUR HATERS

You don't have time to respond to your haters. Don't expel any of your energy on it. If people post negativity, remember it's just a post or a blog but if you respond it becomes a conference. When did Gandhi and Martin Luther King Junior ever stop what they were doing to address their haters? If you are writing a book are you going to stop and say hey let's check with the haters to see if we should publish or not.

We live in America with freedom of speech and anyone can say almost anything they want, I prefer not to ever say anything offensive, I don't like to spread any kind of negativity as what you say reflects your inner world and state, but I am pretty sure it is still not against the law, and we have the power to choose how to react to people's opinions and opposition. Don't waste your time responding to negativity unless it's a constructive post that can benefit you and others. Particularly, do not think or wallow about what others said. DO NOT DO THIS. You are just wasting your precious time. Keep your eyes focused on your vision. Now this doesn't mean don't consider constructive suggestions but know the difference between a hate comment and constructive criticism. Use the advice and ignore the hate. And don't be a self-hater either, that's the worst kind! Remember your worth and your values. Don't let your fears doubt and insecurities stop you from achieving your destiny.

INDEPENDENCE IS NOT THE KEY TO SUCCESS

You can't go it alone. You think you are saving time and money by doing things yourself but in reality that is not the case. You can't grow dramatically unless you work with and use others' brains. If you've heard of the saying, $2 + 2 = 5$, I would take this further and say $2 + 2 = 25$! The total is greater than the sum of its parts because of exponential brainpower and opportunity growth by working together on the same endeavor. This is especially true with a passionate leader who spreads the passion amongst the team with the right work culture. It's really incredible what can be accomplished. Of course you have to structure your team correctly, but once you do, there is no stopping you.

In my experience, when I know things are looking bad and it seems that there is no way out I actually tell everyone things are great and take responsibility of taking the hit on morale myself. Then I figure out the direction to go, prepare everyone and give instructions. You'll be surprised at how things get even better, maybe because we desperately actually need to be hit like that, getting and taking hits in business really is one of the best things because it gets rid of our

154

complacency and puts the team back on tracks. A true leader takes the hits while smiling back to the team, customers and investors. That is why leaders are compensated more financially, simply so they are able to take the hits for everyone else and those finances they are receiving are not meant for self-indulgence and abuse of power.

THE ART OF CREATING

If you worry about what others think, then you will never really create anything. You will unconsciously throttle your mind and your ideas will fail. The mind is a muscle and while our usual ways of thinking provide us with a sense of consistency, in order to create new thoughts, we have to leave the shore of conventional thinking and combine it with childlike creative thinking. If we add responsibility to creative child-like thinking we can truly become masters of our thoughts and start creating things in the adult world.

Let the alternative ways of thinking flow as that lets our brain find new ways of solving problems. Here are some tactics I recommend to tame and master your mind and make it more creative: tame your negativity, seek out what is unfamiliar, and don't be too opinionated because right now whatever you think is the truth, in the future will be ridiculed. Just like most things that people thought in the past, what you think is only a theory and not the ultimate truth. Control what you think, you are not your thoughts rather you control your thoughts which eventually thorough actions have potential to shape everything else in your life. Allow for random positive things to happen in your life as that is what allows creativity to flow. Alternate the mind and be bold and audacious which will force you to work hard to prove people wrong. This is how disruptive innovation occurs. If you want a breakthrough then create deadlines. This will intensify the process while sparking your creativity and intelligence to a new level, giving your process an inevitable boost.

As a creative, you need to alter your perspectives. Don't see the outcome and pattern that fits your past expectations but rather find alternatives and try them out, that's a good way to grow. Don't fall in the same narrow ways and categorized ways of thinking as you have previously. Don't jump to conclusions without paying attention to details. For instance, protestors on the street might be choosing a different side if they looked into the details more about what and why they are protesting. Oftentimes, people don't exclusively study the details, they generalize things and convince themselves that that is the truth, but in actuality with more in depth research they might change their mind. We routinely look for what we already think the truth is ignoring things that do not relate to the way we think or is out of our comfort zone.

CREATIVITY TRUMPS MERE INDULGING

Creativity is often referred to as an evolutionary high-jacking. To be creative is to evolve something out of an old way of doing something. For instance, Uber has evolved the taxi industry and Tesla has evolved electric cars. In other words, take things that are real now or things that have not become reality yet and blend them into something new. That's creative evolution.

Businesses, like life and your mind, are an evolving process where the most innovative and creative process gets rewarded. Evolution is in everything and if you follow this technique you will win in everything. Creativity always trumps mere indulging. We all try to escape reality by indulging in food, alcohol, extreme sports and other activities thinking that this is the way we can really feel alive and connect with reality the most. But truly, indulging brings destruction to our life, not construction. It consumes one of the most precious resources, time, which can be invested into creativity instead. That will produce long-term results and not shortcuts to short term highs that will destruct your life in the long run, and yes this includes excessive shopping or binging on meaningless shows on Netflix.

Creativity or productivity is an ability to extend ourselves beyond conventional and pragmatic boundaries and stale believes in our system that are running our destiny. These boundaries can create stress and unhappiness, however when you switch into a creative state from an indulging state, you will need to make it a habit to adjust your brain and enjoy it. The universe rewards us for the efforts. Indulgence is a shortcut to feel good that is against nature, it releases drugs into your system such as adrenaline, endorphins, serotonin and oxytocin by our brain that are supposed to be released during an actual effort, group efforts, creativity process and many other real life situations. However, because no actual creativity or effort is happening, you have to pay for it some other way like money, health or relationship loss. If you want pleasure without consequences of stress, sickness and guilt that quick fix indulgent brings, then switch to the creative mode where you do something productive and get rewarded naturally. That is what is going to bring true fulfillment and happiness into your life. Again, occasional indulging is ok as long it is done with control and can benefit overall productivity in your life.

CREATIVITY IS THE NUMBER ONE STATUS SYMBOL

A status symbol is some sort of possession used as an avatar of personal worth - it can either be cultural or financial. As such, status symbol can be termed as social cues, just like a peacock's tail. In most occasions, status symbols are associated with financial affluence, although things seem to take a different approach nowadays. In a world that is success-oriented, whether in business or personal development, creativity is beginning to take root as an avatar of success.

However, it is something that most people look beyond without even thinking that it is something of importance. But the truth is that it is the best gift that anyone can have, yet very few will allow it to be expressed freely. Past societies have never really approved of creativity neither did they encourage it to blossom, in fact throughout history creativity has been punished at times. This seems to be fading away with the current and future generations though but not as fast as it should.

Why? Because our societies don't want people to build their own paths to success. For instance, when growing up as a child we were always told what we should do and what shouldn't do by the society. As Pablo Picasso once said, "Every child is an artist, the problem is staying an artist when you grow up." The systems used by schools are to a great extent limiting the creativity of children more than anything else as they focus mainly on a student's ability to memorize things that will be used only for performance at the workplace.

Since creativity is dependent on time most people are often prepared to enter the real world with the decision of getting a job as an easy way out. As such, people continue living life the way society has dictated without thinking about what they can do to make things different for themselves. This is perhaps the reason why at say age 30, people feeling like they haven't achieved what they are capable of in life. It's the reason why most people in Generation Y and some

160

Millennials feel so lost and don't know what to do or what decisions to make.

In today's business world, the only way of attaining the social status that has always been associated with affluence is separating yourself from the pack, and usually not with the GPA you attained in school. The world is constantly expanding with new innovative concepts and ideas. Being able to create something that has never been seen before, whether it's a piece of art or a product, is entirely dependent on how you make use of your mind. However, not so many people are ready to allow their minds to trek outside their cubicles. Instead, they get stuck in them for their entire lives. Not like it's entirely a bad thing.

As Charles Mingus once said, "Creativity is more than just being different. Anybody can be plain weird; that's easy. What's hard is to be as simple as Bach. Making the simple, awesomely simple, that's creativity." By embracing these wise words from the American jazz leader and double bassist, you will be on the right path of creativity and journey to stardom and attaining a social status admired by many.

Create this morning like it is the last one you will ever have. Show up every day and create. You have to completely trust your ability to create. Always welcome new ideas and opportunities. It's a great exercise for your creativity. Fear has to be defeated if creativity is to ever thrive.

INSPIRATION COMES AT RANDOM HOURS

It doesn't matter if you woke up at 4 am, if your mind is not in an inspired, performance and energetic creativity state then your productivity is not to par. That is why it's better to wake up when you are ready and get a good night sleep so you can get the energy to actually perform. It is optimal to get things done when you are creative and in a peak state of rest and inspiration. When genius moments strike, record them or they will vanish. At that moment when an idea strikes the connections between your neurons in the brain align in a way when you have an epiphany and because there are trillions of connections you can't get that moment back. So record it!

Don't be proud of yourself for waking up early if you are not performing. It's a waste of energy and brainpower. Your brain requires power to run so reserve power in other places to give your brain more power for the important task you are after. I can't stress enough of how important sleep is. It recovers our power and brainpower, refreshes your brain, and with the right energy level you will have the right performance level. It's all connected, use it wisely as there is limited amount of energy in the body.

PART

FINANCIAL

BUYING VS. RENTING

There is a lot to think about when it comes to buying or renting, particularly when you own your own business. The real cost of owning a property is forty to fifty percent more than just the mortgage. Also, around 6 percent goes to a realtor. My advice is that if you are buying, be prepared to live there for 5 to 10 years.

Overall, real estate is a poor investment for an individual investor. It's the most overrated investment in America. People are led to believe that they should take a loan from the bank by the very people who want to sell it to you, just like any other product.

From 1890 to 1990 the return on real estate was about 0 %. This doesn't include maintenance or many other factors. Generally speaking, it's a purchase upfront with realized profit much later on. Investing in an all-weather portfolio almost always trumps real estate, although you can include real estate investments within your portfolio.

Here is an example as to why it could be better to rent. Say for example you have 2 million dollars. If you invest the 2 million dollars in aggressive stocks or other investments and you can produce enough income to pay rent, keep the 2 million dollars and then some. OR you buy land, build a house and resell and make quick cash. That's what I am talking about as an example when I say invest into business projects.

BUT if you buy a house to live in, it's a purchase rather than an investment because you can't do anything but wait for it to appreciate for at least 5 to 10 years. And after that time, that money is also eaten up by inflation, plus maintenance and fees and you end up breaking just about even.

Get rid of the belief that renting is throwing money away. Again, that belief is spread by people who want you to believe this idea. The cost of buying, say a $290K home over 30 years with interest, taxes, insurance and maintenance will actually cost you over a million dollars. People say "but the value doubles every 10 years," well yes but also take in consideration that the real estate market is volatile and can crash. Now if you rent a $290K place at about $900 a month over 30 years you only loose around $325K. Again if you invest that difference you have saved from renting into the stock market instead at 8% return rate and compound interest you will get way better results. Houses are like forced savings account; if you put down a small amount as a deposit you also have to pay additional PMI mortgage insurance. So the key is to actually save and invest the cash.

If you really want to buy a house wait until you have cash or very high credit and a good deposit in order to get a lower interest rate. Don't get over your head in a house that you can't afford. Ideally, the price of the house shouldn't be more than three times your annual income. Invest during the real estate market crash or wait for a good deal. But if you don't have the discipline to save and invest the cash then renting is not your best option.

YOU CAN'T BUY SUCCESS YOU CAN ONLY EARN IT

Buying and displaying expensive badges, dining out and traveling to exotic destinations don't make you rich or successful. In fact, it does the opposite. It takes away from time and budget that can be invested frugally into your business to grow your net worth. Although we have been conditioned otherwise by the media and other influences so we can purchase their products or act in a way they want us to.

It's a marketing technique all producers use to put us in a psychological state perceiving that it is prestigious to buy their product and their brands as it can give you a certain elite status. But really, it's just another piece of metal or cloth. A brand is just a psychological state that we are conditioned to by producers of that brand, it doesn't necessarily mean that it is better than something else.

A leather wallet from an unknown brand can be made with the same or better quality for $12 as opposed to a $1,200 high end brand wallet. A car that isn't as a popular brand can have as many options for a better price as a popular brand. Advertisers spend billions of dollars on marketing to hype up their brand so you feel prestige when you are acquiring it and displaying it to others. However, on a molecular level it really isn't any different than any other object that serves the same purpose. Take for example Haagen-Dazs ice cream. They started off as a cheap American ice cream brand and when they weren't doing well, they remarketed as an exclusive, luxury brand that people think is from Denmark. It's the same ice cream, just branded and marketed very successfully with a high end perceived value.

When people move to prestigious neighborhoods they think

they are rich, but actually they become less affluent than if they lived in a lower key neighborhood. Simply because things cost more and not just the mortgage but also gas, product prices at stores and everything around costs more, and if you are trying to compete with or keep up with your neighbors that empties your wallet.

A massive mortgage and car loan does not make you rich or successful. Real millionaires live frugally and invest into assets as opposed to liabilities. They never buy things that loose value as an asset, that's how wealth is created. Even if you are a high income earner you can lose it all really fast if you spend it on liabilities that eat up your cash such as expensive cars and clothes. There are different kinds of assets, some are fast growing and some are slow growing.

The old model is to invest into some stocks and bonds as well as retirement funds but "Wheel chairs don't fit into the trunk of a Lamborghini" as DJ DeMarco puts it in his bold and eye opening book "The Millionaire Fastlane"! If you want to be young and live a wealthy life, invest into businesses and grow them as assets. Get rid of debt and become an investor rather than a consumer. Invest into assets that grow fast and make returns quickly, into your own business, yourself or other businesses such as promising

171

startups. These are all good places to start. Personally, I prefer fast lane investments and I invest into my own business projects.

Whatever strategy works for you is great and I wish you luck with your investments. Just remember you are not rich by liabilities and expensive badges, don't feel the pressure that you have to display expensive things in order for others to recognize your success. That actually makes you less rich than investing into experiences, building skills, relationships and other valuable assets.

CHOOSE BETWEEN SEXY OR RICH

Do you have to choose between being sexy by spending money on luxury items and experiences or being balance sheet affluent (more commonly known as being rich)? Well it really all depends on what you want. You can be rich, be frugal and enjoy life in full all at the same time. Being frugal means you prioritize what you want to spend your money on and you truly enjoy, while cutting back on the things you don't care about or need. All the while saving money for your balance sheet to look plump and healthy.

172

There are two types of rich; income affluent and balance sheet affluent. Income affluence with none or a negative balance sheet is an illusion of wealth and goes away as soon as the income disappears. It's also called living on the edge. On the other hand, balance sheet affluence is the real wealth that can be acquired though exercising frugality, no matter how large or small your income is. If you are an athlete and make seven figures a year and you spend all of it then you have made no progress financially. There are bottles of champagne out there that cost a million dollars so any money can be spent right away without self-control. That's why you have to exercise frugality at ANY and I repeat ANY level of income.

Making 7 or 8 figure incomes doesn't give you an excuse to be stupid and reckless with your money, or you will end up like some of the celebrities out there with millions in debt. People complain and act cheap about the smallest things like gas prices and waste their valuable recourses like time and energy to save a few cents, putting their relationships and other more valuable assets in jeopardy by doing so, while they have other areas in life that if they improve they can save hundreds a month. The reason many people are like this is simply because they confuse being frugal with being cheap.

Again, frugality is when you choose to spend your money on things that you like while eliminating expenses in all or some other areas that you don't particularly care about. For instance, I enjoy nice clothes, but I don't care to travel or buy furniture. This is not to be confused with being cheap which is wasting energy on small puny savings that can actually potentially damage your relationships and quality of life.

This is still a get rich slow approach, if you truly want to get rich then write a book, do a project, invest in a project or business, be creative. Creativity gets vastly compensated in this world, because it reflects the laws of evolution. And yes, you can train yourself to be good at almost any skill, you might not be genetically suitable to be playing in NBA, but rather chose an endeavor that you are suitable for and you can actually reach high results with. Remember, you don't have to be in the top .001 percentile in that skill, you can be top 10-20 percentile and still be successful.

A LOT OF MILLIONAIRES WORK FOR SOMEONE ELSE

There is a very large entrepreneur work for yourself be your own boss fewer currently wildly spreading. But what are the facts? Four out of five millionaires work for someone else, in fact I work for my investors and my clients. And in the case of this book, by trying to provide value to you in a form of valuable information.

How are you going to make money if you work for yourself and pay yourself with money you made from yourself? It requires people to pay you, so essentially you are working for other people; your customers and clients. So now your client is your boss and your investors in a lot of cases. It takes money to make money and whoever is providing it is your boss. If you are funding your own startup, then still when you start monetizing, your client is your boss. You really are never the boss, just concentrate more not on being the rich boss with possessions to display but rather to contribute to others, provide more value on the larger scale with more information and value as that is really what's going to make you successful.

THE ONLY REAL INVESTMENT IS IN YOURSELF AND IN YOUR BUSINESS

Investments such as real estate are not for me at the moment. Long term investments into slow growing assets is preservation of money. Everything else like buying a car or getting credit cards or loans or purchasing many other products is lost money. Unless you are getting a loan to invest into assets that will generate a lot more money than the loan plus payback percentage.

So for me, I invest into myself, my personal skills and personal development as well as my endeavors like my current projects and businesses. That's what has exponential growth opportunity and is not dependent on a bank or economy or any other assets that are out of your control. Take control of your life by investing in yourself, your networks and your business.

PART

6

LIFESTYLE, VALUES AND DEFINING SUCCESS

GROUNDHOG DAY

Five years of experience is not the same as experiencing a year five times over.

Are you stuck in the groundhog lifestyle where every day is the same – you go to work, watch TV then go to bed and repeat? Are you looking for something more? Well, they don't really teach you in school to do more than that.

You have to really dive in and start getting real life experience yourself through your own self-education, working with successful mentors and find out what works best for you. For example, entrepreneurship or building your own personal brand is not widely taught to you in school. But do people care more about what other people think rather than companies? Companies come and go but your personal brand stays for life. Think of many top brands, they are actually someone's name, Armani, Walmart, Ferrari, Ralph Lauren. It's important to cultivate and not suppress yourself.

A lot of the curriculum taught in school these days is hard to apply in real life and is irrelevant unless you are specifically pursuing a career in one of those chosen fields, and if you ever get stuck on a deserted island then you probably don't need complex algebraic equations to survive! For creative types, they teach us proper writing, but when creativity strikes you write from the heart and not according to rules that are suitable for a corporate job. Bestselling books like Harry Potter were not written by taking a technical writing class.

They teach us to wake up early and work at certain times every day, but really your brain is creative at random times. Creativity keeps odd hours so don't be afraid to sleep in and work when you are most refreshed and creative.

We need to rid ourselves of the decades of brainwash that we have received in school or by our relatives and friends for us to stay in the crowd, play it safe and conform. If you get out of the massive brainwash state, you become a leader and people either hate you or love you. If you are different - even if they hate you now, eventually, after getting a following and proving yourself, your haters will follow you as well. This will give you upper hand financially, influentially and open the doors to make a real difference in the world. You can truly make a difference on a large scale as you will have your followers help and guide you along the way. Boldness has power to it.

Become the author of your own life and others will be

inspired by you along the journey.

THE IMPORTANCE OF HEALTHY RELATIONSHIPS

I have been in a successful relationship for quite a while and what I can say makes a successful relationship is full trust, teamwork, understanding and spending quality time together. I can't stress enough how important a romantic relationship in your life is. It is the foundation to a lot of what you want in life and we all know that if you have a bad foundation, your whole house will fall.

I attribute my successful relationship to my giving personality. I enjoy seeing people happy because of me and I love doing things for people, especially my loved ones. Seeing my partner happy because of something I did is important to me.

Also having the same interests and doing things together is important. We are really into a lot of the same things and we spend quality time together doing them. Making quality time for your relationship is hugely important. I am obsessed with my work and spend massive amounts of time working, but again I know for a fact how important spending quality time with my girlfriend is so I do it and put the time in. This is the kind of thing you should be indulging in in your life and not destructive activities as it will help build the foundation of your life.

FITNESS CAN BOOST WORK PRODUCTIVITY

The founder of Virgin Group, Richard Branson, begins his day with a morning run. Anna Wintour, the editor of Vogue, can be found on the tennis court every morning before work at 6 a.m. Likewise, there are a number of highly successful people who habitually participate in some form of physical activity and exercise during the day. What does that tell us? It is a clear indication of the impact physical fitness can have on one's work productivity. The benefits of exercising regularly and staying fit are not restricted to fitting in your dress that you bought five years ago or still being able to pull off your jeans.

In fact, the benefits of exercise and physical fitness extend far beyond that and can give your work productivity a good and solid boost. How? Here are some of the ways this is done:

- **Physical activity keeps you focused and alert**

It is a simple fact that any form of physical activity increases blood flow to the brain, which can automatically sharpen your awareness. A study was conducted and its results revealed that people who are physically fit and indulge in exercise on a daily basis have a consistently high work performance due to improved mental sharpness and better time management. When you are physically fit, you are able to stay more engaged and focused thereby improving your job performance.

- **Physical activity gives your energy level a boost**

Exercising is often the last thing you want to do on some days, whether early in the morning or at the end of the workday. But, research has proven that indulging in physical activity and keeping yourself fit can actually give your energy levels a strong boost. When you exercise, you relieve stress and your body is able to transfer oxygen and glucose throughout. Thus, your energy levels will rise, which keeps you working for longer and enhances your performance.

- **Physical activity improves your brain function**

Your brain can be your single greatest asset, especially if you run your own business or are working with your brain to make money. When you are working, your brain is your primary tool and you want it sharp and alert. Physically fit people do better on cognitive tests as opposed to those who have a sedentary lifestyle. A clinical trial was performed, which determined that there is a clear link between brain function, physical fitness and reduced stress levels at work. If you are physically fit, you will automatically notice an improvement in cognition and mood and overall brain function also increases. With your brain working at full capacity, you are able to concentrate better and focus thereby making better decisions.

- **Physical activity can spark unique ideas**

If you are facing a block at work and find yourself stalled, participating in a physical activity may just help you break through. As soon as you start moving to keep yourself fit, your brain is going to open up automatically and you will get new ideas that you haven't thought of before.

- **Physical activity teaches you to work through discomfort**

Working at a corporate office or running a business can be immensely stressful because you might not get the

184

environment you want. Sometimes you are going to experience some discomfort, but you have to learn to work through it. This can become quite easy when you are physically fit and tend to exercise on a regular basis. It teaches you how to handle pain and discomfort and work through it to reach your goal.

In a nutshell, staying physically active and fit can work wonders for your work performance in the long term.

UNLEASH YOUR INNER CHILD

As a child, when you wanted to do something there was no stopping you until people started to tell you "grow up," "don't do that," "money doesn't grow on trees," and "come do what we tell you instead." As an adult it's even more important to listen to your inner child. Unleash your inner child's creativity and the dreams you once had and go and make them a reality. Find out what you really want, and find a way to make money doing what you love and you will live a very fulfilled life. Be selfish about your passions or others will tell you to stop being selfish and go do what THEY want you to do. If you are going to own your own power stop saying "I don't care" or "it's all good." DO care about what you want and be selfish about your dreams.

As a child, I always drew a distinctive logo everywhere, that I have created in a very specific font and design, the name was Videy. I didn't know what it meant, it was just a creative word. Later I looked it up and it's an island in Iceland that has The Imagine Peace Tower built there. It is a "Tower of Light" envisioned and built by Yoko Ono, John Lennon's girlfriend. On the tower, it says "imagine peace" in 24 languages. And it is lit each year between Lennon's birthday, October 9th, and his death December 8th. Many years later I used the exact design to brand my Technology Consulting firm. When you are a child, your creativity has no limits. Try to recall things you have created or dreamed about and implement them into your life now, I am sure the results will be phenomenal.

Not being clear about what you want, constantly trying to please others or doing what they want you to do will not help you achieve your dreams and your passions and instead you will accomplish theirs. If you don't like what you have or get pushed to do or have, do something about it and change it right now. It might not be as hard as you think. Remember, you deserve to, and you can have everything in your life

186

exactly the way you want it.

Act on your preferences and get what you want, not what you don't prefer and others have told you that you should have or do. If somebody gives you something you don't like then simply explain that you don't like this and that you prefer to do or have what you desire and what makes you happy. Make a list of things you want to be, do and have and act on your dreams, passions and desires and implement them. You can start NOW! Just get up and start taking major actions towards what YOU want in life. Or someone else will use your precious life to accomplish their dreams. Don't listen to what I call 'dream stealers' and don't let them talk you out of your vision. Take a stand right now, it's never too late.

MINDSET LIBERATION

No one is better than you, you are the captain of your soul and all is possible.

Mindset is the most powerful tool in the universe, it can either create or destroy everything, and there are many examples of this though out human history, it can kill you or have you kill other people, it can create life and create everything around us. Mindset is the way your mind is set. So, if the way someone else is or thinks or does things is not the way your mind is set, then you don't have to kill them or oppose them, instead try to understand why they think that way. All conflicts come from differences of mindsets, the way your mind was developed with experience and content exposure during your lifetime, sadly it's part of the natural selection process, to eliminate or oppose people with different points of view. So, in order to liberate yourself from this natural selection process of constant fight and opposition of others you have to unset your mind from one frequency and into unlimited frequencies. Accept all possibilities.

Everything around us that is man-made is a result of the way of thinking and mindset configurations. The way you act and clothes you wear, the way you act at graduation ceremony versus at a concert or at a nice restaurant or at the beach, all of it is a result of our thinking. We can simply act any other way we want during that particular event or wear or not wear anything, we can build a house out of trees that grow outside for free and give it tremendous value, we can earn a diploma and act so proud when we receive a piece of paper, we can wear certain designer clothing or jewelry that cost us a fortune, when jewelry is just dug up rocks on one side of the planet and sold on the other side for tremendous value, who says that it is valuable, because it shines? Well you can see the world around us as not a big deal, as only we make it a big deal, that is how to liberate your mind, don't start acting crazy and weird and get arrested please, but just know inside that you can do or not do anything or say and not say anything wear or not wear anything at that moment, important things are made important by us, in ultimate reality no one truly knows what the ultimate truth is, we only act accordingly to how our brain chemicals are released at certain situations, but that isn't the ultimate truth.

A lot of things, sayings and content around us exists simply to put and bring masses down to conforming level of running away, settling down, staying quiet, not standing out, obeying and going to work for others, because people with power are aware of the power of the mindset and they use it on others, because they don't want to perform hard, real work and use you to produce product and service for them while you stay quiet, and they want you to do it willingly. For instance, you ever heard people say these things or caught yourself saying them: maybe I shouldn't say that or maybe I should do that, that's embarrassing, that's too much, you probably shouldn't do that, no it's not going to work, it's not the way it is or should be, that's not what I've heard, you should be ashamed or embarrassed of yourself, you should be doing this exact thing by this exact age or you are wrong or a looser, you are weird for doing or not doing this, where are those believes coming from, really, who says that's the way it is?

School system books exists mostly to train your mind to perform work, not to benefit for yourself or learn how to become the leader of the world, and if you are trying to benefit for yourself or gain something, they call you selfish, ignorant, greedy, narcissist and many other names. Well if you are a bit selfish that is fantastic, do things for yourself, help yourself, secure the gas mask on yourself first, in fact how can you even make an impact or help others if you are not helping or sustaining yourself first. Liberate yourself from the cage of society, product and celebrity placements in movies, shows and sports to tell you how you should live, from dictatorship of formal education, buying things and doing things that are getting pushed on you every day. Do what is good for you, and what you want to do, benefit for yourself.

Also speak up and stand out, don't be afraid of anything, don't break the law or harm other people but there are really no other limits. If you want to wear something wear it, if you want to say something say it, if you want to do something do

190

it. Remember nobody in this world is better than you or are the authority on how things ultimately are, nobody has more authority, power, smarts and education than you because it's all made up phycological level stuff that in ultimate reality is insignificant, we are all the same, authority is man made by those who want control and power, to succumb to it, badges, diplomas and certificates are created to give authority and make some people look or feel better than other people or motivate them to perform certain actions or work, as well as to monetize and make people pay in order to get that badge that they tell you, you need to buy in order to get to the next level when really self-education and repetition of skill you want to learn is what you should be doing. Be the authority of your own life and doings. If you don't have a degree, it doesn't make you less smart than the person that does, if you dress less good or have smaller house in a less prestigious neighborhood, that doesn't make you less rich or less important.

If you want to become somebody big you simply can by authorizing yourself or training that skill, but really you don't have to, you will still be as good as the person who did become big or great, everyone is unique and doesn't need badges to prove that they are. Nobody is better than anyone else, nobody has more authority over you, you are the captain of your life, your doings and your sayings. The people who really become of power, success, get big following and are influential all have one thing in common, they are not afraid to speak and do what they want to accomplish. And others, who think less of themselves, which is only on a psychological level, follow them and think that they are the boss simply because their charisma is overpowering them. So, the way to become so called big, overpower everyone with your charisma, be super bold and confident in what you say and do, and yes dress and carry yourself also, the whole image matters, and make it THE way, what you say and do is the way and the way it should be, that's what gives authority. Nobody really knows what is THE way is but confident people push it to the limits repeatedly no matter of others opinions, so others have no choice but to follow them because they think if they are so confident at what they say and do then it must be THE way and must be true. Big leaders and many other bozo brainwashers on YouTube and so many other recent fake self-authorizing, self-branders are not opposed as easily, because media and their followers back them up, then they must be right, right? Well, let me tell you, nobody in this world knows exactly what is going on, no one is the real expert ultimately, it's all just talk, gurus are

192

marketing themselves to give themselves authority to make it look like what they are saying is valuable to monetize on people and charge more. So, remember no person is above you no matter who they are, it's just another guy constantly going to the toilet, remember all big leaders also have to wipe theirs butts, and by just knowing this you can reach any level and authority in life. Don't ever think of yourself less than any other butt wiping person. You are the universe, you are the world, you can create anything, you can do or not do anything, you can say or not say anything, life is in your hands, you are the master of your life internally, nobody else is. Liberate your mind and be or not be anything you want.

FOR REAL CHANGE, START WITH YOUR FRIENDS

"I'll be there for you!", - theme song from the show "Friends".

Your environment and who you surround yourself with is one of the most critical aspects of your success. If you want to make a real change in your life and progress towards your dreams, the first step is to get rid of your friends that you are currently hanging out with at least for a while. If you are not where you want to be in your life, then people who you hang out with and vibrate your mind though either with by just being around them will always drag you down like crabs.

I want to share this story with you. There is actually a type of crab whom fishermen try to lure into cages with a food bait. All of the crabs come into the cage and they start eating so the cage is closed and they get caught. Sometimes the food runs out in the cage but the crabs are so used to the food being there even though it isn't there anymore they stay in the cage. Once in a while there is one crab that realizes there is no more food in the cage and he tries to crawl out but the other crabs are so convinced that there is food still there that they stay in the cage and try to stop the other crab from leaving. If the crab persists they even sometimes try to kill him.

The importance of this story is to be the crab who tried to crawl out. If you know something to be true follow that and leave the people behind who don't support you. Similarly, if you are doing something different, they will not understand it or be concerned and try to oppose it, as it is natural for beings to try to bring people higher in hierarchy down for their own safety.

When you have a habit of say drinking with particular friends the habit is always triggered around those friends. You accumulate a number of unhealthy habits and beliefs as a member of a certain group of society. You have accumulated and associated with specific friends during certain periods of your life while implementing same activities. If you want to go on a different level stop what you are doing and do something else. You have to pause or stop your close relationship with them. Of course, if you are currently satisfied with your life situation, your current friends are perfect because they share this current mindset with you.

Dramatic change really requires you to be selfish and do what you know is right despite anyone else's opinions. Your comfort zone and persisting with the same way of thinking will not get you to the next level of living and your current friends oftentimes are your comfort zone. They will try to tell you that your current life is the only way to live, but there are people that live way different lives, just as you are aiming for. I am not saying they live a better life, simply if you want change, it will require social change in your life as well. If you expose yourself to likeminded people, your mind like a sponge and will start soaking up their positive energy. You don't even have to speak with them, just being around other minds that are vibrating like radio waves on the same frequency will do the trick. So be careful whom you vibrate your mind with.

DON'T LET DOPAMINE, SEROTONIN, OXYTOCIN AND ENDORPHINS IN THE DRIVER SEAT OF YOUR LIFE

These are chemicals released by your brain that are responsible for rewarding us for certain behaviors. However, if we are not careful we can abuse their powers instead of using them for the purposes they were meant to be used - as guidance in our system. Many events can trigger these neurotransmitters, but rather than being addicted by the feel good feeling we get from them, we need to be constantly aware of what is happening in our body and do what is beneficial to us as evolved humans. If we strictly chase the next short term high, we become like rats in the lab pressing the buttons.

Dopamine motivates you to take action toward your goals, desires and gives you pleasure when you are achieving them. Procrastination, self-doubt, and lack of enthusiasm are linked with low levels of dopamine. By being aware of this you can raise your natural level of dopamine by positive thinking, exercising, listening to music and many other healthy and natural activities. I don't think I need to reiterate how important it is to get rid of procrastination, self-doubt and lack of motivation in business.

Serotonin flows when you feel significant and important. Loneliness and depression are there when serotonin is absent. That's why some people fall into criminal activity because the culture and 'community' or sense of belonging to a gang or a group that could perform negative or positive actions together releases serotonin. On the other side use the presence of serotonin to boost your sense of creative and positive community, family and workplace teamwork creation.

The release of oxytocin creates intimacy, trust, and strengthens relationships. It is released by mothers during childbirth. Oxytocin is the glue that binds together healthy relationships. Use the knowledge of its presence for building relationships with your clients and team at work, in your family and your intimate relationship.

Endorphins are released in response to pain and stress, and elevate anxiety and depression. Which are very common in modern society. Some factors like drinking and other unnatural endorphins release feelings that contribute to elevated anxiety and depression. Without endorphins to get us going, like the 'runners high' phenomena, we would not be striving and doing things over and over. Endorphins get us to get things done. Remember that when at work, sometimes overworking is an addiction so taking healthy breaks is important. Along with exercise, laughter is one of the easiest ways to induce endorphins. So laughing and staying positive is a great way to keep the natural way of endorphin levels high.

After raising self-awareness with these neurotransmitters, you can truly realize that either they are using you with addictions and negative behaviors, or you can use them to build a great life and business.

Crocodiles' reptilian brains have no reward system in their brain that provides reward for cooperation. If two crocodiles launch at prey they have no sense of cooperation of achieving that goal. We are not crocodiles. Although we still have a primitive portion of the brain, the evolved brain we have has adapted to help us work together in cooperation. That's why you need to apply it at the workplace to build cooperation with other evolved minds in order to achieve a common goal.

THOUGHT->ACT->HABIT-> CHARACTER->DESTINY

A lot of thoughts we have are not always correct because they are inspired by personal opinions, emotion, prejudice or fear. So control your thoughts with will power. Everything starts with your thoughts, which eventually shape your destiny. Use self-discipline and the power of concentration and apply it to your thoughts. You have complete possession and control over your thoughts. At any time, you can change them from negative to positive, instantly. Control your negative emotions by transmitting them into constructive action and use them as inspiration. Use positive thoughts and emotions for the attainment of the definite end of your desired goal. All this is accomplished by establishing habits of thought. Faith without discipline is just a dream and the ego used positively is the driving force to accomplish meaningful things. With discipline, your faith and ego can be directed in both your business and personal life to reach the highest achievements possible. You can think yourself into or out of any circumstance of life and you can convert every failure into an asset.

Thoughts become things. In fact, positive thoughts that are

beneficial to what you are trying to accomplish help you to want to push your thoughts into things that would otherwise remain as just dreams. The more positive action you take, the better. Even if you fail you should look at it as motivation to do more and better and learn from it to improve your strategy. That is why more action is better. Don't stop but rather take action after failure simply because at this point you are more knowledgeable and your chances of success are higher.

Habits are like ropes they are viewed with threads of action. If you combine aligned and inspired action from positive thoughts you will build great habits that will become automatic, like going to the gym or performing work tasks without procrastination. We are what we repeatedly do and habits make us who we are. Habits are like exercising a muscle, they get bigger and stronger with more repetition. Simply keep repeating positive tasks with your conscious mind and your subconscious mind will pick them up as a habit and will start performing them automatically. Forming correct habits is very crucial for one's success in life and business as it builds character. By creating positive characteristics, the universe picks up your intentions and starts working for you. If your intentions align with the universe you will be greatly rewarded. Because your destiny starts with your thoughts, look within yourself for your own success formula – make an elaborate plan, take disciplined action and build positive habits. It's all in your hands!

Our attitude is shaped primarily by our beliefs. We all have multiple belief systems and we have beliefs influenced from parents, close friends etc. We are constantly bombarded with images every day of how much money we should make, how we should look and we often set those goals for ourselves but they are not our goals. Your beliefs really do shape your goals so it is important not to define your goals from the beliefs of somebody else if it contradicts your own beliefs and values.

The beliefs that we are getting bombarded with are beneficial to those who are pushing them on you, so they can sell you their product and service and take your money. A lot of things around us exist for that sole purpose. Have your own agenda and don't fall for others' agendas. Don't spend your most valuable asset, your time, and your budget on what you got pushed into believing by others. I think, and it makes me sad, that mostly the younger generation is constantly the victim of this, and people who know how to brainwash the masses use this technique to get rich on you and persuade you into actions that are forced beliefs by commercials, repetition and many other methods.

Approach the achievement of your goal just as you would begin any journey; with a very specific destination in mind based on your own believes and values. Your goals need to be something that you want and are not pushed upon you by others. They need to be realistic and achievable and you will need to remain persistent and patient in order to realize them. Be aware that there will be obstacles and setbacks during the process. Successful people expect obstacles and see them as boosters for better performance. The key is to be resilient and not let your minor setbacks hold you back. Set up milestones and celebrate minor milestone achievements with rewards while you are moving towards your bigger goal. And as we've touched on previously, always come back to your Why.

ASSETS FOR SUCCESS

You may be asking yourself, how do we look at success and how do we define it? Here are my top 10 tips for success:

1. Moderate your eating and drinking and other self-indulging activities

2. Speak positively to others and think before speaking,

or reacting

3. Maintain a sense of order and ensure everything has its place and schedule, break down your daily schedule to minutes not only hours

4. Be a finisher and commit to finishing what you have started

5. Work hard and efficient, optimize your time

6. Be sincere and practice integrity in everything you do

7. Maintain justice and don't do people wrong. Remember the Law of Attraction: what you put out, you attract and get back

8. Maintain balance and learn to let things go

9. Be resilient and calmly accept minor setbacks or small misfortunes, don't let small defeats defeat you permanently

10. Learn from mentors and books. Study carefully what successful people have done and learn from their experiences and failures.

EMOTIONAL ASSOCIATIONS

I have said it before but here is it again. Almost everything around, is designed to attack us on a psychological and neurological level in order to squeeze money out of us in any way possible. Companies and brands use neuroscience to release drugs produced by our brain into our system to put us in the state where we are vulnerable enough to make purchases.

Everything at the corporate stores is designed to extreme preciseness to trigger the right purchase at the right time, like snacks are placed at the end so when you are a bit more tired by the end of shopping you will be more lenient to make the unhealthier purchase decision. When you walk in a high-end clothing store, the service, music and design are all targeted for your brain to release drugs into your system to feel high and important to shell out a little more mulla.

Higher education hype is the biggest scam of them all, we are brainwashed from childhood that it is prestigious and necessary to acquire badges of education to get a good life for yourself so we are pushed to pay top dollar for prestigious schools.

All this hype exists by corporation leaders who want you to become a corporate slave because you have to pay for your student loans and you need a secure job. The same thing goes with credit cards as banks want to make money off you by tricking you into certain promotions, points and many other bells and whistles which again release drugs by our brains into our system because we are getting money up front when in reality they are the ones making the real cash. If you opened up a nice growth saving account you feel like you are making money, but the people who are charging you fees are the ones.

It's one big system where people at the top control the masses financially, make them work for them, produce the product and make money for them, like the Egyptian self-proclaimed gods used to make slaves build the pyramids for them. This system has existed for thousands of years, and was very big in the 20th Century during the industrial age. But now we've hit the connected informational age, where the so called top dogs are losing the grip, because first of all there are people like me who read and desire to tell people the truth instead of keeping secrets for selfish benefits. This kind of integrity is starting to get rewarded in the connected age as brands don't own people anymore, people own the brands.

Sharing information now is promoting products and is getting compensated greatly in the connected age, like doing gadget reviews. The better information you share the more you get compensated because people see integrity and reward it. We start sharing rides, even possessions, our houses (just look at Airbnb), and also our thoughts. It's a non-selfish approach that will definitely bring the human kind to a better future and fast.

WHAT IS PRESTIGE?

Prestige means something different to everyone. Here are some key commonalities associated with prestige

- Communicating exclusivity, achievement and value

- Earning admiration

- Being ambitious and focusing on being better

- Results oriented and having very clear specifics of what you want

- Respected over the achievement

- Being positioned as aspirational and being out of

reach for most people

- Elite and spending more time or working harder to get what you want

- Showing and displaying to the world what you value

- Increasing perceived value or setting a new standard

ADDICTION IS SIMPLY A PRACTICE OF BAD HABITS

When you put thousands of hours into doing something your mind is adopting that skill. But a lot of people practice negative skills like indulging in food and alcohol, playing computer games, watching TV, while they are not extremely bad habits, they are not particularly the best investment of your time if you want extreme success. If you practice your mind to do something positive you can take baby steps and retrain your mind to get in that mode and be healthy with those habits instead.

In the same way, recovering from addiction is incremental and you can expect setbacks. Don't be defending your obviously destructive behavior. Ignorance of its existence will lead only to its continuation and making it stronger with more repetition.

When you exercise addiction, it comes from putting a lot of hours of practicing it over and over again. For instance, computer games trigger chemical releases in the brain because you get a sense of accomplishment similar as what you would get in the real world with the results of delivering a project or achieving something, as you complete a quest and get a reward. Our mobile phones are an addictive device as they give you a dopamine release. Once you exercise this enough in your mind it becomes engraved and it's hard for your mind to retrain itself into developing a good habit like going to the gym, because it's occupied with the feel good of the buzz you get when you get a Snapchat message.

So how do we beat addiction? Well any type of small progress is the key. You eat an elephant by taking small bites. Just start biting. Push yourself several times and your brain will start being accustomed to that action instead. People are afraid of addiction and label it like they are punishing themselves. Don't do that. It takes time to retrain your mind to develop good habits and get rid of bad ones. Training the mind is a slow process and just like a muscle, you can't get buff right away as it's hard work.

not to, as the amount of their actions shows the results. Don't concentrate on perfection rather concentrate on sales, actual customers, and actual results. Stop burying your wants and desires. If you want a perfect marriage or to be rich or famous, be healthy and have a perfect body. Don't let others tell you "just be grateful for what you have," being grateful is great but don't be a victim of others telling you to conform and settle. Remember there is almost nothing to be afraid off now in the modern age especially in America, my grandfather fought in World War II and I guarantee that every one of our problems now is nothing compared to what those veterans went thought and the difficulties they have faced to win freedom for us. It is precisely because they didn't give up and produced actions and not excuses that we have a fantastic way of living today. So what are you doing to leave a legacy and make our future generations life great?

BRAGGING IS GREAT - IF ITS TRUE GIVE YOURSELF CREDIT

"It's not bragging is you can back it up!" – Muhammad Ali

Bragging as a negative term was created to make people

conform like communists to not stand out and accomplish more for themselves. Well, communists actually were motivated by songs and other effective propaganda to work harder. Did you know that current music is chosen by not it's creativity but how it gets reacted by your brain, that's why some songs are stuck in our heads, because the industry knows which tunes to play over and over again, and while you are in an emotional state products are getting pushed into your subconscious?

Conditions like ADD, hyperactive and other are considered illnesses and to be treated with medication by doctors to calm you down to the mass conformity level. Prescription drugs are a huge epidemy in the U.S. and it really has become a problem, I think this topic also needs to be addressed and raised awareness for.

But actually bragging (in a humble manner), same as hyperactivity and even ADD and some other so call illnesses can be and are often the way to more action, more accomplishments, a more outgoing personality and more creativity. All these things can lead the way to riches and prosperity. And people that know that, don't want the masses to exercise them, so prescription drugs and brainwashing is implemented on the mass scale to stop and go run away and

212

settle down, get mortgages so you have to work and make the bank rich, produce babies and get pets to buy products for them, and purchase product from the rich, who are creating product and making money on you, so you are nice and ripe to give them money while being afraid to be creative and outgoing yourself. I know I am repeating myself a lot, but repetition is what gets people to truly understand things as subconscious picks it up, I explain this process in the book in several chapters to bring awareness. And you know when I was younger I thought all this subconscious and conscious mind stuff is a bunch of kumbaya, but after reading several scientific books written by people who studied these phenomena's and explain it in the rational sense, I started to understand how it really works and how to really apply it into my personal life, and it works. So that is why I am eager to tell others as well, so people can use this knowledge to their advantage. Think of all richest people, actors, entrepreneurs, politicians, they didn't listen to anyone telling them to play it safe or talk it down. Don't listen to people trying to drug you down and telling you that you have a major problem. Instead be creative and outgoing. These creative and hyper types of influencers spark conversations at the water cooler and on social networks, give great speeches throughout history of human kind, and they get a following because they have

213

personality that isn't afraid to challenge the status quo mentality. Spark conversation, innovate and be creative. That is what's most rewarded in this world and always will be.

STOP LIVING IN RETREAT - FOCUSED ENERGY

Be frugal with your brainpower. A brain is lazy and likes to conserve energy by taking the easy path whenever possible. In order to conserve energy, don't focus on the areas of your life that are not on your priority list, instead be obsessed with the areas of your life that you are pursuing. This will give what you are chasing more dedication and energy, more productivity and directed action towards your main goal. The results will speak for themselves. I deprive myself of energy wasting on unimportant tasks and information, like watching Game of Thrones or listening to gossip in order to give large bursts of energy to my brain at the times when I need to produce results in the endeavor I am after.

ALWAYS STRIVE TO BE AND DO MORE

Invest into yourself, your own personal development and always strive to be and do more. Don't just run back to your safe cave after performing one task for the day. Keep building and keep growing. The final result matters, not the fact that you have tried and did something as nobody cares that the process is hard. Instead, achieve the actual results.

Don't let your old barbaric part of the brain dictate your modern lifestyle. Instead train your neo cortex to evolve, and no, watching TV doesn't train neocortex, it trains the barbaric brain with all the violence, sex and other triggering emotions packed into shows and movies. If you want to train the frontal lobe, read some books, find mentors, go and implement creative action, don't consume and repeat what others have made, create content and product from your mind. The value is in creation.

YOU ARE WHAT YOU CONSUME

You are what you mentally consume. We are surrounded by TV shows, apps, movies, music, news, politics, sports and advertisements and are bombarded by content that is keeping us in the state of barbaric brain firing up and being active, that's why people get emotional, loose their cool, yell at other drivers and get in arguments with others especially after a couple drinks as that further indulges the barbaric brain, this is all anti-evolution like. Instead you need to break out and train your evolved part of the brain with content that is useful and will put you into a productive and creative state. That will change your mindset, which will change your life, if you want to be successful your mind has to be in the productive state as opposed to the consuming state. All this massive content exists around you for a single purpose to trigger your barbaric brain to buy, and rid you of your money so you have to go back to work for the same people who rid you of the very same money and it's a never-ending cycle.

HOW THE BRAIN WORKS AND HOW IT ASSOCIATES WITH OUR BUSINESS ROUTINE

The human brain operates like the Internet. When you type a The human brain operates like the Internet. When you type a phrase or a word into a search engine site, it, as a result, brings up a range of information related to what you have typed in. Similarly, the brain brings up the information that may relate to your knowledge, experience and your individual interests.

A brain is continuously bombarded by approximately 2,000,000 bits of information per second. This means you need to start getting a better perspective of why you might need some kind of reminders every day. In fact, a brain can't deal with this collection of information and so it gets rid of the huge accumulation of what it receives. This shows that you are usually left with 134 bits to cope with.

In simple words, your nervous system is not able to cope unless it sorts the details this way. All this suggests that since you can only cope with a limited number of information at any one time, it is very important that you concentrate on the right actions only.

Seeing that, stress has a great association with different aspects of a business, many businessmen feel a great deal of overwhelm and it's just the way of life. However, it can take lots of essential energy away and make you feel sick and frantic and even cause the whole brain to blank.

Business owners have a lot going on in their life that often makes them feel that they will never acquire the success they have always dreamed of. This not only leads to poor productivity and procrastination but also puts the owners in a situation where they feel the need to engage psychiatrists for effective ways of dealing with their anxiety and stress. Usually, these physicians prescribe them anti-depressant medications that are effective in addressing stress but also act as a band-aid effect and don't address the core issues.

The neurotransmitters or brain chemicals are responsible for the information exchange between the brain and cells. Three of these neurotransmitters are vital for human conversation: serotonin, dopamine and adrenaline. In simple words, they are "feel good" neurotransmitters of the human brain. Anti-depressant medicines cause abnormalities in the automatic motor system; a large cluster of nerves found deep in the oldest part of the brain. When your brain attempts to pay off for the side effects of a medicine, it can lead to several disorganized and chaotic activities such as lazy unconsciousness, confused mind and feelings of panic.

The brain is a very complicated part of a human body and experts are still trying to find out its functions to the full extent. Although doing so is a huge challenge, there's a mass of information that's discovered by more advanced imaging

218

and scanning methods that highlight what is happening inside the brain as it carries out certain functions.

The complexity of the brain also requires experts to have a comprehensive understanding of the science to be able to apply it effectively and carefully to a business as it can otherwise misrepresent ideas and draw wrong conclusions. However, there can be several powerful ways to tie your own power together and put a stop to the energy draining cycle. You can start with jotting down everything that's running inside your brain. It's important to discover what business tasks and priorities are important for now, and focus on them only.

SURROUND YOURSELF WITH THE RIGHT PEOPLE

Surround yourself with people who can contribute and add value to your life and not just are there to benefit for themselves.

The people you invite on your journey or as I say on your bus, are the most important to your success in life. Make sure you have the right people. Some people cannot go all the way with you so be selective. Choosing the right partnerships in life is a huge factor. I can't even describe how much I personally use this strategy in life to succeed. Anyone that I work with or do business with I choose, because after years of working with people and businesses I can tell who is going to be a pleasure to work with and we can actually be successful at our project. On the other hand, I know whose mindset is coming in with a negative attitude even before they get started.

You will need others for resources as you can't get big objectives done without the help of others. I personally like to hire and work with people who are smarter and better than me to learn and grow for myself and to ensure the success of the endeavor.

Don't forget to bring your skills into the fight. Know your skills and use them in the right situation. Know your strengths and weaknesses and work on your weaknesses when you are working as a team, don't ignorantly believe that you are the best or you are not wrong, just take a look at what you need to work on to improve it and then truly become better.

Sometimes people confuse ignorance with being optimistic. Know the difference and you will grow and improve in areas that need improvement. Create partnerships with people who possess different strengths than you have and together you can complement each other to full success and learn and grow from each other.

THE ONE ABSOLUTE AND TOTAL SUCCESS FACTOR

The one total success factor is maintaining absolute and total self-confidence no matter what people say or do to oppose it. This is how disruptive innovation occurs and is at the core of evolution and the meaning of life.

I want to share this one strategy because it worked for me all my life. The only thing that really matters is having absolutely no doubt in your endeavor and the absolute confidence in what you say and do without. Once you no longer need to look externally for an approval, that makes you the source of leadership and people will follow your vision.

YOU CAN CHANGE YOURSELF INTO ANYTHING YOU WANT TO

You are the creator of your own reality which means that you create your personality, habits, money situation and other things in life by wiring and rewiring the neurons in your brain.

We are absolutely free to wire our mind the way we want it to be regardless of our background or current situation. We don't have to rely on the survival mode anymore. We are in a new era of creation. We don't live in a cave world anymore. If you haven't practiced doing or being who you want to be go and practice it a few times, neurological pathways will be created in your brain and that behavior will become automatic. When you make the behavior you want in life automatic, you will create the exact life you desire, including the amount of money you want and any other personal and happiness goals.

NEGATIVE STATEMENTS TO WATCH OUT FOR

Here are a couple of key negative statements that entrepreneurs and successful are often told. It is good to recognize them and know that you are not alone if confronted with them.

Stop being so ignorant - imagination and creativity is something new. Out of this reality, you create something out of nothing, so if you are not ignorant of your current reality how are you going to create and inflict disruptive innovation?

Don't bite off more than you can chew - Dwayne Jonson once got told this but he said that he would rather choke on greatness than live a life of mediocracy. Again this is up to you as no-one is pushing you to do anything. We are not our brain and we can control it with willpower. If you want to relax go and do it, if you want to take a vacation go and do it, if you want to keep on working just do it.

Don't be selfish - if you can't take care of yourself how are you going to take care of others and make an impact on the world? If you don't make money how are you going to help your loved ones, help those less fortunate and do the work you were called to do? You need to take care of yourself first and don't label it selfish, label it as a philanthropic prerequisite.

Just be grateful - being grateful is great but it doesn't mean that you don't want to strive for more. Be hungry for change and challenge and helping others. It is important to grow and have wins for yourself and your family but don't confuse the state of gratefulness with just being grateful for what you have.

There are many different hidden statements to watch out for, so what I would recommend is to stay positive and remember the haters are only trying to make sense of the decisions that they have made in their lives. Oftentimes, negative statements are people projecting their own insecurities onto you.

WE ARE WHAT WE REPEATEDLY DO

The 10,000 Hour Rule —by writer Malcolm Gladwell. The principle holds that 10,000 hours of "deliberate practice" are needed to become world-class in any field. I have read some of his books and highly recommend checking out this great Author.

Being somebody is what we have thought and practiced so many times that it requires no conscious will to activate. That can be revived by thinking and doing things that you want to become, or the way you want your life to become. So anyone can become anything by repeating and practicing thoughts and actions that are a prerequisite for their goal. For instance, Olympic athletes practice the move so many times in their mind and body that it becomes automatic. You can do that too, you can practice something and think about it and the more you do that the more it becomes automatic. You can practice performing negative tasks like smoking and it becomes automatic as your thoughts trigger that action and then you go and implement it into actual action, which becomes your life. But you can control it. You can switch your thoughts to different thoughts that are productive and positive and implement those thoughts instead.

It is also extremely attractive to have willpower and self-control implemented positively into your life and become financially and physically fit. For reproduction, the opposite sex is looking for those who have evolved their brain and body to that level of achievement and it is very attractive. Because the genetics do mutate during a lifetime of a successful person in a successful way and financially and physically it shows. But if you are negatively evolved with negative thoughts and actions you are not attractive for reproduction because genetically your brain and body didn't evolve to be suitable for future generations to have a better chance of evolving in a better environment and with a better genetic code.

DO IT YOURSELF OR HIRE OTHERS?

I used to just hire everyone to do work for me, anything I can hire for I did to liberate myself from doing it and so I just delegated tasks to other people. But is that a good move? Yes, and no. My psychology always was to delegate tasks to others while you can concentrate yourself on things that matter most like marketing, client acquisition and sales. Yes, this is a great strategy but it's greatest challenge is to get other people do the work correctly and to care, because if it's not their endeavor they truly deeply don't care enough.

I always was and still am facing deadline problems and the speed with which you can keep up with your WIG (Wildly Important Goal) are always jeopardized by the mere factor that other people care to get paid for what they do but not give it all they have got. This is almost always the case with employees. It's very hard to find someone who truly cares about the work itself. I truly care about the work itself and I care about people. When I am doing the work for my clients, even if it's not my project it becomes a piece of me and my life and is very exciting for me to work creatively on other people's ideas.

I think that's what got me to be successful in business in the first place. But like I said earlier, delegating tasks and taking on more work and more tasks gets challenging because employees often are not emotionally engaged in other peoples' dreams and vision. I personally think striking a balance is great, always trying to look for those people who have a genuine heart for what they do and I can see it right away during the hiring process as that is what I have and what I am looking for in people I work with.

Sometimes I have to take matters in my own hands and end up doing it so much faster than actually paying someone to do it. Then I wonder why I've wasted so much time trying to find the right team and people to complete the task when I can train myself in that skill so fast and get it done better. So I suggest for those who are just starting up a small business to try doing things themselves as sometimes it is a better route and with so much information available now these days you can train yourself at so many tasks and fields.

You are the person that cares most about your task. If you find people to work with who are lightning fast and care about the work as well then don't let them go! Reward them and let them know that you know that they are thriving and are deserving of great compensation. I often offer bonuses to people that I've worked with for a long time who are fantastic. So, build a caring team, keep them at all costs and reward them as much as you possibly can, but still try to accomplish tasks that you can learn fast yourself because nobody else will do it better than you.

LIFE CHANGING MOTIVATIONAL QUOTES

Over the years, I have read, researched, done business, spoken with and learned from some of the best. I am a highly driven and motivated individual and personally, I love to create and listen to motivational quotes and tips to get me and others inspired. This chapter is designed for you to refer to when you need a bit of extra motivation to get you going! I am going to leave out who it's by, as everything has been said before, and repeated and created in someone else's mind somewhere else across the globe at a different place and time. Most of these I have wrote creatively from myself or from materials I have heard or read before, if you want to look it up you are welcome to. So, at this point it's more important to soak up that information and apply it into your life and lives of others to create the better good.

- Don't let perfection be the enemy of great. Just do good work and get it to market as quickly as possible so you can collect feedback from users to innovate it to their needs

- Large companies like a person who worked in a startup because that individual understands innovation

- A start up is a marathon, not a sprint

- Pluralistic ignorance is when people go alone with something because others agree with it

- Don't always use money as an enchantment tool. Sometimes a great cause succeeds without funding

- Before you react, seek first to understand

- Have no doubt in your mind of who you are and your reality will reflect it

- Put that spirit of knowing there is more to life into your product and service

- In order to fly we need to have resistance

- Successful companies start out to be successful not to make money

- Failure is not due to outside factors, its mostly internal

- Whatever you do, do it with passion to benefit somebody that is not you

- When you stop being like other people they stop liking you and that's ok

- Don't let the noise of others opinion drown down your inner voice, heart and intuition

- The true achievers are born at challenging times

- Don't live with the result of other people's thinking

- If you work hard on your job you will make a living if you work hard on yourself you will make a fortune

- Each person's income is determined primarily by their philosophy

- The bigger the dream the more important is the team

- Most people operate at a fraction of what they are really capable of

- Time is so vital that you might use a stopwatch to train yourself to do your most vital work and not waste a second on anything else

- Focus means not saying yes but rather to say no

- Every time you say yes to something you are actually saying no to something else

- It's not what you learn or what you know it's what you do with what you know and learn

- The key to success is to fail massively

- Ignorance and entitlement ruins business. Yesterday's wins wont fuel tomorrow's wins.

- If you feel very uncomfortable you are doing the right thing

- A strong stand is what will attract you super fans

- Fear – use it don't let it use you. Build courage to face it head on

- Knowledge itself is like sitting in a Ferrari but failing to push the gas. Actual action required.

- Insanity is doing the same things repeatedly and expecting new results

- If you have to think about affordability you can't afford it

- Life doesn't begin on Friday night and end on Monday morning

- Smart men learn from the mistakes and wise men learn from others' mistakes

- Stop climbing the pyramids and start building them. Most people struggle financially because they don't know the difference between an asset and a liability. Rich people acquire assets while the poor and middle class acquire liabilities that they think are assets.

- More money doesn't solve problems – intelligence does

- Winning means being unafraid to lose

- There is gold everywhere most people are not trained to see it

- Find a reason greater than reality

CONCLUSION

I wrote this book not with a goal to monetize it or market myself, my brand and my business, like I have realized a lot of books are doing after reading so many. I wrote this book, to better understand what I have learned from life experiences, reading and my deepest thoughts and share it with others, because by writing it down is how you really truly understand the meaning of what you have learned, better yet by telling it to someone else. That is also why I made an audio version, where I tell it in my voice with as much passion and emphasis on the parts that I think are especially important for you and for many other people, who I hope will use this information to their advantage in life and pass it on to others to also better their lives, that way we are all making an impact together. I have a burning desire to share and contribute to others what I have discovered from my own personal experience and knowledge accumulation, either it's trial error in business, success stories, brain structure, philosophical outlook on our purpose and existence, or just good old motivation. I applied this creativity and ended up with this book.

I also desire to be a public voice where I can help influence and make a difference by speaking out to make positive impact on the world on a larger scale than my own self benefit. My genuine passion for contribution and pouring back into the world has been there since I was a child and I really wanted to put it into action and make an impact for many years and I really hope I did it with this book at least if you are reading it now, I have made the difference. I believe that this is the key to a life of happiness, to me at least, and I hope this book will help spread that feeling that I have to others and also trigger the good side of them to keep spreading the passion and positive actions towards others furthermore. I hope to awake that positive loving person in everyone who reads this book as everyone has that in them. I hope they will pass it on to others to start thinking and acting in a positive way and the rewards coming to them will truly be unimaginable as that's what aligns with the laws of the universe. People who align with those forces in a positive way will be rewarded regardless of any obstacles they face in their path.

I want to thank you, my friends, for reading this book where I have genuinely and passionately tried to express my experience and knowledge in my career in business, personal life and many books I have read and many things that I have realized. I hope you use it in your personal life as building blocks together with other positive information and experiences to impact your life, life of your loved ones and the world in general. I wish you all best in your business and life journey. Liberate your mind and soul and think, do and be anything and everything you can conceive.

Made in the USA
Middletown, DE
15 January 2021